THE PSYCHOLOGY
OF
EXCEPTIONAL FISHING

Jay T. McNamara PhD, LP

Preface by Denny Brauer

The Psychology
Of
Exceptional Fishing

**Copyright © 2007
By Jay T. McNamara, PhD,
Licensed Psychologist**

Published by Bass Edge, Inc.

ISBN 978-0-9794671-0-3

Cover design by Don Hertz

Cover Photo of Author by John V. Austin

*Printed in the United States of America by
Morris Publishing
3212 East Highway 30
Kearney, NE 68847
1-800-650-7888*

DEDICATION

This book is dedicated to Corrinne Marie Bedecarre, whose love, intellect, encouragement, and ideas made it all possible.

THE PSYCHOLOGY OF EXCEPTIONAL FISHING

Preface by Denny Brauer

Introduction

Do your Homework

Set the Stage for Success

Action Steps

Special Topics

Acknowledgements

Fishing was first: Lake Rebecca, the Mississippi river, and the St. Croix. Psychology came later, in Missouri, Alaska, California and Minnesota. Eventually the two would flow together and become this book.

Along the way, many people contributed ideas, support, and inspiration. Chief among them are:

Paul and Corrine McNamara, who got me started, fishing and otherwise;

Brian McNamara and Dave Haas, my earliest fishing partners;

The Canada Crew, Tony, Ron, George, Floyd, Mark, Jay, John, & Mark;

The Creek Orthodox Alaskan Brotherhood, Slim, Newt, Oscar, Roy, and also Stump;

The guys from Denny Nelson's Mystery Lake tournament circuit who showed me the magic in competitive bass fishing, Randy, David, Brad, Denny, Kurt, Pat, and especially Loel, my mentor;

My most fun fishing partners, Dorothy, Patrick, and Ellen;

My fishing heroes, Denny Brauer, Rick Clunn, Tommy Martin, and Larry Nixon;

My psychology/psychiatry mentors and partners, Gary Blackmore, Rex Blake, Gary Burger, Bill Clarey, Iris Cornelius, Peter Flint, Steve Kahn, Dennis Kelly, Glenn Lewis, Jim Martin, Loring McAllister, Ann Meissner, Mary Melbo, Doris Read, Keith Shaw, Hal Steiger, and Peter "Jewboy" Zelles;

The people at *FLW Outdoors*, especially Leanne, and Patrick, my editor;

The West Metro BASS Club, especially Steve, Carroll, Bob, Jason, Pete, Rick and Catfish;

The teachers/writers who showed me that "Beauty *is* Truth, Truth, Beauty", Richard Pearl, Dr. Joseph B. Connors, Ted Trueblood, John Geirach, and Herman Mellville;

My consultant from *Bassmaster* magazine, Louie Stout;

The folks at Target who taught me about leadership, including Dave Biron, Paul Dominski, Mitch Stover's Distribution Operations team, and Tiffany Scalzitti's Distribution Human Resources team;

The *Bass Edge* staff, Don, Mike, Glenn, Matt, John, Jeanne, Diana, Jacob, Jennifer and most especially to Aaron Martin, who also believes that "for some.... nothing is written";

My transcriptionists, "CJ" Johnson, Sue Ribe, and especially Beth Burrus;

The *one guy* who believed in this book before I did, Glenn Hirsch, PhD;

And most of all, Tom "Wally" Wittkopp, the best fishing pal a guy could ever hope to have!

PREFACE

Jay T. McNamara, PhD, LP combines his knowledge of Psychology with his love of fishing to create one of the most helpful books ever.

Jay has spent many days fishing with me around the country. He is an excellent angler who continually strives to become better. During our days on the water, we discussed the need for a book like this. I have known for years the importance of a positive mental attitude for success. I have tremendous confidence in my ability, and in the decisions I make on the water. It was not always that way. It took years of hard work and dedicated effort to develop a winning mental edge.

In this book, Jay gives you great ideas and exercises to shorten this learning process. There are so many situations you deal with in fishing, especially competitive fishing, and many of them are negative. Losing fish, breaking lines, interference from other anglers, the list goes on and on. The better you handle these negatives, the easier it is for positive events to happen. If you follow Jay's advice, your fishing will move to the next level.

The Psychology of Exceptional Fishing will make beginners as well as experts better anglers.

Thanks, Jay, for taking the time to give the angling world your expert advice and knowledge.

Denny Brauer
Camdenton, Missouri
January, 2007

Introduction

Welcome to **The Psychology of Exceptional Fishing!** In the following pages you will find descriptions and examples of how performance psychology principles can help you become a better angler. While this book may be especially useful to anglers who compete in tournaments, the concepts and principles apply no matter how or where you fish.

You are probably already familiar with stories about how athletes in other sports use performance psychology principles to be more effective. Golfers have popularized the practice of visualization. Professional baseball, football, and basketball players also comment on the importance of concentration, confidence, and mental preparation.

Additionally, Olympic athletes around the world have used sport psychology principles for decades to achieve peak performance. More recently, competitive anglers are recognizing the role that mental or psychological variables play in tournament success.

To be sure, this is not a book about psychological theories. **The Psychology of Exceptional Fishing** emphasizes practical exercises you can use every day to improve your effectiveness.

You will also find a **BIG** emphasis on making performance psychology exercises fun! Fishing is supposed to be a good time, right? Getting psyched up or mentally prepared to fish should be enjoyable as well.

If you have pursued this sport for even a short time, you have no doubt seen in yourself and others how mental variables can positively as well as negatively affect results.

You wouldn't intentionally go fishing with dull hooks or frayed line, for example. You try to come to the lake as physically well-prepared as possible. But do you consistently use all your psychological resources? The several pages of exercises that follow will help you answer that question in the affirmative!

You will find this book valuable if:

- You have ever lost a fish (and money!?) because you weren't paying close enough attention;
- You have made poor decisions based on lack of confidence;
- You let anger and frustration squash your fishing efficiency;
- You catch fish in practice but "tighten up" and fail to execute on tournament day;
- You race from spot to spot, without a clear game plan;
- You have trouble getting "up" for competitive events on waters where you have done poorly in the past;
- You used to catch them, but feel you have lost your "edge;"
- You feel disruptively torn between multiple commitments. When you are on the water you think about what you should be doing at home, and when you're home, you are constantly thinking about fishing!
- You have already been "In the Zone", where *everything* seems perfectly aligned!

The Psychology of Exceptional Fishing will address these and other common issues that both tournament and non-tournament anglers face. As you read, keep these ideas in mind.

First, remember times when you faced other new activities such as learning arithmetic, mastering a musical instrument, or playing a new sport. To become skilled, you needed a lot of practice. Even something as basic as learning to read took time and effort. And, while the "See Spot Run" series might not have seemed helpful at the time, eventually your hard work paid off. You would say the same thing about acquiring other skills such as learning to drive, or figuring out how to hit a baseball.

Getting the most out of Performance Psychology skills will be like that. Some of the techniques illustrated here may be unfamiliar. However, learning them *will* make you a better angler. If you're not convinced, call or write to top tournament guys like Rick Clunn, Mike Iaconelli, Larry Nixon, Kevin Van Dam, or Denny Brauer. They might have a thing or two to say about the mental side of fishing!

Additionally, a primary focus of this book will be helping you create your own mental training program. By understanding your unique personality, temperament, and learning style you can build a set of mental exercises tailored to *you* and how *you* fish. Therefore, this book can be helpful no matter where you are or where you want to go in your fishing career.

As will be quickly apparent, I am clearly biased toward obtaining baseline information prior to making changes. Tournament pros, for example, talk about the importance of knowing what size fish you need to be competitive on a given body of water. Similarly, you have to know what "normal pool" is on a reservoir to tell whether today's water level is up or down. To that end, several exercises focus on helping you understand where you are *now*. In fact, self-awareness, or self-understanding is such a key variable that you will find multiple opportunities to catalog your skills, traits, values, priorities, commitments, and goals. At some point you may say to yourself "This exercise is pretty similar to the one I did a few chapters ago." And you will be correct. Like multiple casts to high-percentage targets from different casting angles, good psychological exercises are worth repeating in different forms. You can't tell until you try it which exercise, or cast, will be the one that works!

Of course, not all of the principles and exercises in these pages will apply to every reader, and some techniques may seem awkward or unnecessary, especially at first. Feel free to pick and chose what works for you and what doesn't, though at least experiment with these ideas before you toss them aside. Treat this as a workbook and utilize the tables, graphs and worksheets sprinkled throughout. My goal for you, as you will read in **Chapter 19**, will be to help you create a unique **Psychological Tackle Box**, a personalized set of mental tools that apply specifically to you and your fishing situation!

Also, **The Psychology of Exceptional Fishing** is designed to introduce you to many performance psychology principles, and show how these can be applied to the world of fishing. In each chapter, I will present a few exercises that illustrate how these ideas can be put to work. This overview is not designed to cover any one topic in exceptional depth, however. Entire books have been written on subjects like time management, visualization, and mental rehearsal.

As I will describe in **Chapter 23**, the most effective use of these techniques would be in collaboration with a sport psychologist, someone who could help you create, in a hands-on way, your own **Psychological Tackle Box**. Think of it this way: if a friend wanted to take up bass or walleye fishing, you could give that person a book that would explain basic baits and presentations. However, it would be far more helpful to take your friend to a tackle store and explain and sort through the maze of colors, sizes, and types of lures on the shelves. Similarly, your friend would do well to have you or someone else demonstrate how these lures work rather than just read stories about where and how to use them.

Still, you have to begin somewhere, and my hope is that **The Psychology of Exceptional Fishing** will start you on the path to learning how mental techniques can improve your angling effectiveness. Most of the examples I use in this book refer to bass fishing, with a particular emphasis on competitive bass fishing. However, the same principles apply to walleye, crappie, muskie, or saltwater anglers. Regardless of the species, if you want to fish better, these techniques can help you.

TOOLS

In order to maximize your results, you will need the following tools:

- A three-ring binder filled with lined paper which you should label your **Psychology of Exceptional Fishing Notebook**.
- An 8-1/2 x 11" calendar, or a *FranklinCovey Day Planner*
- Pens, pencils and magic markers/highlighters

As you read this book, please fill in the graphs, use highlighters to underscore things you like, and write notes in the margins; whatever you do, don't just sit there and read without getting involved. That would be like trying to learn to ride a bicycle by reading *Cycling News* magazine. Experimenting with and practicing the exercises in this book will be the mental equivalent of time on the water.

At the end of each chapter is a **REGULAR GUY TIP**. These are for anglers who think mental exercises are too complicated or too much work. At the very least, try the **REGULAR GUY TIP** and see what happens.

There is an important constraint I need to tell you about. Unlike other writers, I am bound by professional confidentiality statutes, as a psychologist, not to disclose the information people have shared with me in confidence. I can only tell you what specific anglers said if they have given me permission. As a result, many of the examples I will use throughout this book will take the form of "According to one top pro....", or "One angler I worked with told me....." I wish I *could* tell you exactly what individual pros have said, but in many cases I can't!

One final thought. Look at the fish I am holding in the cover photo. Catching my one and only legitimate seven pound Minnesota largemouth bass was directly related to learning enough about the mental side of fishing to think through where that fish would probably be and what she might eat before I caught her. Once I began fishing tournaments, I discovered how to harness the psychological principles that allowed that picture to be taken. And believe me, if I can do it, so can you!

CHAPTER 1

Commitments and Priorities:
Get Your Mind Right!

Performance psychology techniques will be most helpful if you start with being clear and specific about your priorities and commitments, particularly those related to fishing. It might be tempting to skip this chapter, since you may already feel solidly invested in a competitive tournament career. However, do yourself a favor and explore this commitment issue anyway.

Consider this key concept: Whether you realize it or not, a serious commitment to fishing occurs alongside many other important priorities, including commitments to your family, your friends, and your community. Also, your priorities are likely to reflect commitments to your faith, personal values, and perhaps to sponsors. Most individuals also have commitments to outside jobs as well.

You may *believe* you can be happy living in your truck or van while you eat, sleep, and breathe fishing. You have no doubt heard stories about pros who sacrificed everything for their angling careers. Before following in their footsteps, however, be realistic about what you are taking on, and about the sacrifices required to pursue your commitment to fishing.

Don't get me wrong. I'm all in favor of chasing dreams (I wrote this book, right!?). At the same time, in order to be good at any one thing you will need focused commitment, the kind that will preclude or diminish other activities. Therefore, be clear with yourself about what those other activities are, and where they fit on your priority list.

On balance, conventional wisdom is in line with psychological research suggesting that an inclusive perspective and a long-range timeframe are more effective than a shortsighted, restricted focus. Recognizing and balancing *all* your priorities and commitments increases the likelihood that your dedication to fishing will work out.

Exercise 1: Establish Priorities

In order to put your fishing commitment into a realistic context, you should spend some time exploring your personal situation.

Using your **Psychology of Exceptional Fishing** notebook, or the table below, review a typical week. In the first column, list all of the different things you did that week and how much time you spent on each one. Include regular things like eating, sleeping, doing the laundry, etc. If you fish tournaments, you might want to do this exercise twice, once for a week during tournament season, and once for a week in the off-season.

The important thing is to be inclusive. List all of the activities you typically pursue. Then write down the approximate number of hours per week you spend on each activity. Remember, there are a 168 hours in a week, so that's your benchmark.

Spend a few days thinking about this exercise to make sure your list is comprehensive. Also, ask a friend or relative to review your list for accuracy. Above all else, be honest with yourself! If you can get by on six or seven hours of sleep, fine, but if you really need eight, don't cheat on the sleep number. It will catch up with you, I promise.

In the second column, write the ideal number of hours you would like to devote to each activity. Now comes the important part--reconciling column one and column two.

For example, let's say you spend 25 hours per week with family activities, when ideally you would like this number to be 30 or 35. What categories can you borrow from to make up the difference? Similarly, if your ideal number of fishing hours is 20, and you currently only spend 10, you may need to make some difficult choices.

Once you have finished this exercise you will have a good picture of the activities you value the most. These are your priorities, the things to which you are committed.

Exercise 1: ESTABLISH PRIORITIES

Activity	Time Per Week Now	Time Per Week Ideally

Exercise 2:   Annual Review

This commitment exercise is worth doing on an annual basis. Regardless of where you live in the country, there is an off-season when you can spend time reviewing and adjusting your commitments. In the same way you regularly schedule maintenance for your truck and boat, you need at least an annual review of your priorities and commitments to keep them aligned. So mark today's date on this page in your **Psychology of Exceptional Fishing** notebook, and designate that same day on next year's calendar to review this exercise.

Exercise 3:   Commitments for the Future

Many of the tournament anglers I talk with don't want or expect to compete at the same level forever. Eventually you may hope to join the *FLW Redfish Tour*, or fish the *Master's Walleye Circuit*; or maybe you want to win the *Bassmaster's Classic*! This next exercise will help you think about your current commitments in a larger time frame

Use the next table, or your **Psychology of Exceptional Fishing** notebook to write down where you would like your fishing career to be in three years, five years, and ten years. Feel free to dream big here. For this exercise don't worry about whether your dreams are realistic or achievable, just write them down.

FUTURE FISHING CAREER

Three Years:	
Five Years:	
Ten Years:	

After you have listed where you want to be in three, five, and ten years, write the names of three or four people you know who have successfully reached this level. Let's say, for example, that you are committed to competing at a national level within five years. Very cool! Instead of just moving into action on your dream, find a way to contact nationally successful anglers and hear their stories about how they turned their dreams into reality.

It's like being a teenager and thinking you want to be policeman when you grow up. Before you make a firm commitment to such a career, it might be helpful to talk to a few law enforcement professionals to find out what it takes to become a cop, and what the life of a police officer is like.

Name	Contact Info. Phone numbers, Addresses, etc.	Comments

Books, websites, and career counselors can be helpful, but really nothing beats talking to someone who has already made it. Hearing what others have gone through to realize their dreams will give you a better understanding of what you are up against.

This exercise will require effort and creativity on your part, but it can also be great fun. You could, for example, go to a national tournament, introduce yourself to your favorite anglers, and ask for a few minutes of their time. You could also write to, or e-mail some pro anglers and tell them your story. Be candid and politely ask them to give you their version of what it takes to be a competitive angler.

When I was just getting started in tournament angling I did that myself. I guess you could say I was naïve in thinking that guys like Larry Nixon, Tommy Martin, Guido Hibdon, Denny Brauer, and Rick Clunn would be willing to take the time to talk to someone like me. However, as I discovered about professional anglers generally, these individuals are genuinely nice guys, and happy to talk about fishing! You will also likely discover this universal truth: Most people enjoy talking about themselves and their careers, especially those who have been successful. Just don't expect top pros to talk much while they're fishing! The following story will illustrate what I mean.

As you may know, I have been writing a column, **Performance Psychology and Tournament Fishing**, for the *FLW Outdoors* web site for several years. The photo in that column series was taken of me fishing out of Tommy Martin's boat during a rainy February day on Sam Rayburn Reservoir. A fishing magazine article led to a phone call to the former *Bassmaster Classic* champ about a possible fishing trip in Texas. Being the nice guy that he is, Tommy talked with me on the phone for over 30 minutes about lures, techniques, and patterns we would be using. My reaction was something like, "Wahoo, this guy loves to talk! I will learn so much from a day in his boat!" We made the trip to Hemphill, and Tommy was equally expressive as we drove to the lake. Once we hit the water, however, he was a changed man; intense, focused, and *silent*! At one point he did say, "Let's try another spot.", but that was essentially it until we put the boat on the trailer, whereupon he turned back into the talkative, gregarious guy I had encountered on the phone!

So talk to pros away from the lake, and when you do, use your **Psychology of Exceptional Fishing** notebook to keep track of what they say. You needn't be discouraged by horror stories you may hear of how hard it is to make a living at fishing. Clearly, however, a long-range commitment based on a realistic perspective is more likely to work for you than one based on sketchy information or naïve idealism.

Take managing money, for example. Most pro anglers will admit they *seriously* underestimated the expense side of their fishing careers. Yeah, I know, you probably think you're different, that you're one of those guys who are very realistic, accurate and frugal about how much cash goes into and out of your fishing fund each month! Okay, well, here's an opportunity to prove you are right, and I'm wrong.

In your **Psychology of Exceptional Fishing** notebook write down, for one month during fishing season, *every dime* you spend that is in some way, shape or form related to fishing. The rods, reels, and terminal tackle you purchase will be easy to notice and list. So will the money you spend on gas and oil for your boat. However, as every professional angler will tell you there are a zillion "hidden" costs associated with a fishing career.

For example, make sure you write down *all* the money you spend on fishing trip food and beverages, including the stuff before, during, and after each trip! Remember, it costs money to operate and maintain the vehicle that tows your boat. As of this writing, 39 cents per mile is the tax rate for vehicle use in a business, so keep track of your mileage, and see how much *that* adds up to in a month!

And I don't just mean trips to and from the lake; include mileage to and from the local tackle shop, to and from your buddy's house to plan the next trip, and back and forth from the marine dealer, or your trolling motor repair place. At the time you buy them, a few bucks for swivels and sinkers, or a ten-spot for a couple bags of Senkos doesn't seem like much, but if you honestly keep track, you will probably be *unpleasantly* surprised at month's end!

At the very least, your own calculations will provide a realistic sense of what you spend currently. Then you will be able to blend this information with the expense stories you hear from pro anglers to understand what your financial commitments might be if you decide to pursue a competitive fishing career. This financial data, along with what you have written about your other commitments will give you a balanced picture of how fishing fits in with *all* your priorities!

7

REGULAR GUY TIP

Even if you don't do all those exercises, at least do the money thing.
Keep track for a month during fishing season of everything you spend
on fishing and see if you can realistically afford this amount. If you
are married or live with someone, discuss with your domestic partner
how fishing expenses fit in your joint budget. If you don't, you may
pay Big Time later!

.

CHAPTER 2

Practical Skills First:
The One With the Best Cast Wins (Usually!)

Let's get one thing straight. Being a successful tournament angler requires a solid foundation of practical fishing skills. All the visualization and relaxation exercises in the world will be a waste of time for someone who makes poor presentations with the wrong bait in a bad spot! To start with, you need a realistic picture of where you currently stand.

Exercise 4: Practical Skills

Use your **Psychology of Exceptional Fishing** notebook, or the accompanying table, to make a thorough list of the specific skills necessary to be a successful angler. The skill list below is not complete. Remember, *your* set of practical skills will be different from those of your friends. However, this table is a great outline to get you started.

Consider doing this exercise with fellow competitors, and compare your ideas about what practical skills are necessary for fishing success. Collaboration can make this exercise more enjoyable as well. Once again, be comprehensive. When you have completed your skill list, grade yourself on each one, A, B+, C- just like in school!

Keep in mind, if you make an error in self-assessment make it in the negative direction, at least for this exercise. Giving yourself an 'A' when you are only a 'B-,' is a mistake, and here's why. To begin with, you will be fooling yourself into thinking you're better at something than you really are. On principle, that's a bad idea. Ed Zern, the famous fishing humorist, once wrote, "Fishermen are born honest. But they get over it." That may be true, but try to work around that idea when evaluating yourself! I interviewed several tournament anglers prior to writing this book, and the most common mental mistake they described was anglers *overestimating* themselves.

Also, if you overestimate your skill set you will miss opportunities to improve. Ultimately, you end up believing you have developed certain skills you do not yet have. On the flip side, if you give yourself a 'C,' even though this underestimates your skill level, you are at least in position to learn more about this dimension. When it comes to evaluating yourself, keep in mind the words of Rick Clunn, recently voted World's Greatest Angler. In Rick's view the *best anglers* are only a 5 or a 6 on a 1-10 scale, at this stage in our sport.

Also, you should have both general and specific skills on your list. Casting accuracy, for example, is not just one thing. Specific skills in that category might include flipping, pitching, and skipping docks, in addition to general open-water casting. Using soft plastics also includes several subcategories such as Texas-rigged worms/craws, jig worms, lizards, and so forth. As I said, the chart below is not complete. Ideally you will use it as a starting point to make a detailed list of the fishing skills you desire. Once you have graded yourself, pick three of your lowest grades and make a commitment to improving them.

Exercise 5: PRACTICAL SKILL DEVELOPMENT

Skill	Grade Today	Skill Development	Final Grade
Boat Control			
Sonar Interpretation			
GPS skills			
Navigation/Map skills			
Fish Location skills			
Strike to Land Ratio			

Casting Accuracy			
Presentations:			
Spinnerbaits			
Shallow Cranks			
Deep Cranks			
Soft Plastics			
Jerkbaits			
Jigs			

Practice Plans

It may seem obvious, but I'll say it anyway: learning new skills will be easier and more efficient if you have a practice plan. Trial and error can be a reasonable teacher, and there's a lot to be said for experimentation and learning on your own. In fact, you're probably already pretty good at self-instruction. (I'll just bet you didn't need six weeks of coaching and an instructional videotape to learn how to ride a bicycle!) However, many fishing skills are quite a bit more complicated than bike-riding, and with complex tasks, a practice plan can be an effective guide. Let me suggest you use this three-step practice approach:

1) Analyze
2) Modify
3) Execute

Here's how it works. Let's say you want to improve your jig fishing. Since Step One is **Analyze**, you should begin by looking at your current approach to jig fishing. Start with your rod, reel, and line. Examine what you use now, and then check out books, articles, and web site chat rooms where you can compare your equipment to what other anglers use. While some people use spinning tackle to fish jigs in open water, you'll probably find that most pros use medium-heavy or heavy casting rod/reel outfits, especially for heavy cover. Additionally, you may find a few chat room discussions about monofilament versus braided line, and you may enjoy experimenting with both to see what works best for you. Some anglers get carried away at this point and start buying all kinds of new equipment, though you needn't jump the gun here. Take your time and find buddies who will let you try what they use before making major purchases.

Now consider the jigs themselves, and the trailers that go with them. Here again, use multiple sources of information to compare your choices to what others suggest or recommend. Internet chat rooms are especially fun and interesting because you will get a wide range of opinions on this topic, from the sublime to the absurd, as they say! However, when evaluating your equipment, nothing beats going to a fishing tournament, either as a participant or spectator, to see firsthand what top anglers use.

Besides evaluating your equipment, you should also analyze your techniques. Ideally you would use your coach here (See **Chapter 22!**). However, if you don't have a fishing coach, ask a couple of individuals who are known jig experts to share their approach. E-mail correspondence, phone calls, or parking lot conversations after tournaments can all be useful ways of contacting technique experts. Experimenting with different methods on your own, plus information and suggestions from others will increase learning efficiency. It says here what you already know, that learning complex tasks *from someone else* is more efficient than a trial-and-error, self-instruction process.

Step Two is **Modify**, and that means making some changes in your equipment and/or your technique based on what you have learned. Don't be afraid to experiment here. As mentioned earlier, while some use braided line for flipping jigs in cover, many people report they prefer heavy monofilament. So rig up two outfits, one with mono, one with braid and compare them head to head.

Also, experiment with what you find out about trimming skirts and weed guards, and try different trailers as well. Yeah, I know, you'll wreck some baits, but so what? One angler I know spent an entire summer fiddling with jig size, skirt and weedguard configurations, and various trailer setups. Conservatively he messed up over a dozen jigs that had to be thrown away. Was it worth it? I'll let you decide. The last tournament of the season he used his newly designed jig to catch a limit that weighed *twice* what the second place guy had.

Step Three is **Execute**. Here you need to get out on the water and use your newly modified equipment and techniques enough times to get comfortable with them. I can't tell you exactly how many hours, days, or weeks this will take. Sometimes you come onto a new technique, and it's like meeting an old friend; instantly you get a comfortable, familiar feeling, and you just know *this is it*. Other times it takes longer, and you may end up back at the drawing board, so to speak, making additional modifications until you have the combination that feels best in your hands

The most important thing is to highlight specific areas that need improvement and then work on them. Give yourself 2-3 months in each area, and then see what progress you've made. Use the right hand column on the chart to assign a new grade. If you still fall short of your expectations, commit to another 2 months to improve that skill!

REGULAR GUY TIP

When other people offer advice or suggestions, use your head and rely on common sense! For example, what is easier to bend, a short stick or a long stick? Duh! So when you trim the weedguard on your jig, don't make the bristles shorter, and therefore harder to bend! Instead, clip weedguard bristles completely off, two at a time, until its right.

CHAPTER 3

Know Yourself:
Who Is That Person Who Lives Under Your Hat?

Accurate self-understanding is a foundational dimension for peak performance. It goes without saying that even if you have the best lures and a state-of-the-art boat, you are at a clear disadvantage on an unfamiliar body of water without a good map. From a psychological perspective, having an accurate picture of yourself is just as important as knowing the contours of a lake.

For example, do you recognize and understand the basics of your temperament, or personality? Do you know your primary learning style? Can you list the advantages as well as the risks associated with your unique approach to competitive fishing? Do you recognize and anticipate stressful circumstances, or people who upset you? Are you aware of what motivates you or makes you happy, and do you understand what calms you down when bad things happen? Having answers to these kinds of questions can make you a better competitive angler, as well as a better person. Let's look at how this works.

There are several paths to self-understanding. Personal reflection, information and feedback from others, or a formal personality evaluation by an assessment expert can all help you understand your primary characteristics. Later in this chapter you will find an exercise to help you know yourself better. For now, consider these two important psychological dimensions: temperament and learning style.

Temperament

Temperament essentially represents the personality you were born with. Each person's personality is made up of several interrelated traits. You are probably familiar with basic personality dimensions such as introversion and extraversion, for example. Some of us are highly outgoing and rarely shy. Such individuals want and need to be around people. These are the extroverts. Others are reserved, and interpersonally they prefer to fly beneath the radar. They enjoy spending time by themselves. These people are introverted. Many of us fall somewhere between the extremes of introversion and extraversion, at times exhibiting characteristics of both.

Knowing where you rank on this personality domain, however, can have important implications for a career in competitive fishing. For example, if you are highly gregarious, you may find studying and practicing psychological techniques easier if you work with partners. Similarly, if you are extremely introverted, you will likely want and need time alone to experiment with different mental exercises.

Recognizing your place on the introversion-extraversion spectrum will make it easier to manage other aspects of your fishing career as well. In teaching psychological techniques to anglers over the years, I have had heard numerous personal tales. One story that repeats itself nearly every season is about the tournament rookie who camps out by himself, far from his fellow fishermen. Such anglers tell me they are imitating their fishing heroes, guys like Rick Clunn who are known for physically removing themselves from the frantic social atmosphere that surrounds tournaments.

If you are a private person like Rick, this may work for you. As a reserved individual, you will naturally feel comfortable by yourself. Being around too many people for a long time can tire you out. However, it is both painful, and at times funny, to hear obviously extroverted individuals talk about the stress of operating in isolation. Gregarious individuals need frequent contact with people, and the more outgoing you are the more social contact you will require. Too much "alone time" for an extrovert can make you tense and irritable. Affiliative, outgoing fishermen would be much better off with a roommate (or two or three!) in a motel or campground close to tournament headquarters!

At another level, would you say you are principally a calm, unruffled individual, mostly a passionate, excitable person, or somewhere in between? Since self-evaluation is notoriously unreliable, ask a few friends or colleagues to offer their impressions of you. Knowing where you fall on a calm-excitable scale can certainly help your fishing career.

Typically, calm people are less emotionally affected by successes and failures than excitable individuals. Being calm makes it easier to remain focused if you lose a fish, or if equipment breaks down. However, a calm, low-key individual may be slower to react to bad situations than an emotionally intense individual. One angler I know takes busted equipment in stride, so much so that his stuff stays broken way too long.

Excitable, emotionally driven individuals are almost always on the go, and when problems arise they move fast to correct them. However, such persons are also at risk to react too quickly, making changes before they have thought through what they are trying to accomplish. Such individuals make more than their share of careless mistakes as a result. You may be thinking that your partner who wants to change spots four times in the first hour of a tournament is an emotionally intense individual, and you would probably be correct.

Excitable people rarely have difficulty getting "up" for competition, though in multiple day tournaments, and over a long season, the intensity such individuals exhibit can be draining. It's difficult to remain in high gear indefinitely. Similarly, while calm, emotionally-contained individuals may be slower out of the blocks, they may be steadier and more emotionally consistent over the long haul.

Learning Style

One way to understand your primary learning mode is to think about how you most often take in and retain information. Using a new lake as an example, are you most likely to remember a particular spot if someone tells you where it is, or if someone shows it to you on a map? Depending on your answer, you may principally learn by hearing, or you may prefer to learn visually, by seeing new information.

Obviously each of us uses all of our senses in interacting with the world, though research tells us that we each have a preferred or dominant sensory mode. Many successful competitive anglers are exquisitely skilled in the art of visually processing information. The capacity to see and quickly make sense of several pieces of visible data is a huge asset in our sport. Reading tides and currents, noticing and understanding underwater structure, and observing cues in the natural environment are of obvious value, and these will come easily to the visual learner.

If your primary learning mode is visual, most likely you will prefer a "show me" approach to new information. However, you will probably not be surprised to know that predominantly visual learners may have trouble remembering information which is heard but not seen. Such people often make it a point to carry a notebook to write down information they hear.

Alternately, you may already have strong listening skills. You are the kind of person who hears something once and remembers it. You can take advantage of your good listening skills by asking questions, engaging in conversations, and paying close attention when others offer advice or suggestions. Similarly, in order to be a successful tournament angler, you may need to do practice exercises to sharpen your visual skills.

Let's think about learning in another way. Consider the difference between a conceptual approach and a practical one. Going back to that new lake scenario for a minute, when you look at a lake map, do you quickly envision spring, summer, fall, and winter fish-holding spots? Do you look immediately for public accesses and channel markers? If so, you may primarily use a practical approach to new information. Many good competitive anglers are this way. However, an overly practical orientation can have limitations. You may, in this example, not spend much time wondering about who made the map, or when it was plotted, information that could have important implications for accuracy.

Another type of person might wonder about how the map was constructed, or about whether the lake is a highland or lowland reservoir. This person may have more of a conceptual approach to learning. Academic types, those of us with advanced degrees, have this tendency. However, I can tell you from personal experience it can be a real distraction to get overly conceptual or theoretical during a tournament!

As is likely apparent, there are advantages and disadvantages to whatever your temperament and learning style might be. However, I'm not talking good or bad here. Instead, I'm suggesting that an awareness of who you are can improve your approach to fishing. Knowing whether you are right-handed or left-handed has implications for how you fish boat docks, right? The same thing applies to other personality characteristics; the more you know about yourself the better you will fish.

Do Your Inventory

You frequently inventory your tackle to make sure you have everything you need. Here's a chance to do your personal inventory. Use the following table to make a list of 25-30 words or phrases that apply to you. Ignore the second, third, and fourth columns for now and just focus on describing yourself. Use adjectives such as optimistic, friendly, private, resilient, determined, adventuresome, courageous, thoughtful, or cautious.

18

You can also write phrases like risk-oriented, quick-witted, slow to anger, committed to family, easy-going, and so forth. As with other exercises, use friends, fellow anglers, and relatives to make your list accurate.

Exercise 6: SELF-AWARENESS

Words that describe me:	How does this trait help me?	How does this trait hurt me?	How do I change this trait?

After you finish this list, set it aside. A few days later, pick it up and check to see if what you have written is accurate and complete. Once you have a clear picture of the person who lives inside your skin, spend some time reflecting on what you have written. This is who you are. These traits and characteristics have gotten you where you are today, so take a few moments to say "Thanks, pal". In later chapters, I will talk more about the importance of self-acceptance, though this is as good as any place to start.

Now, let's put the rest of this exercise to work. In the second column consider how each trait might be helpful to you. Focus primarily on how this trait benefits your competitive fishing, though if you notice other areas of life were this dimension is valuable, write that down also. If you have "good father" in the left-hand column and you can't think of how this might help you net more fish, write down how this helps you at home.

In the third column, jot down ideas about how each characteristic might hurt your competitive fishing. Here again you might not initially think of anything for some traits. Fine, not to worry. However, you might also notice, as others have found doing this exercise, that a few characteristics can help as well as hurt your fishing career.

Before you move on to the last column, ask a close friend or relative for thoughts and suggestions about your inventory. If you do not already have a sport psychologist, this exercise is one where a professional can be extremely helpful.

Finally, using the last column, make notes about how you might modify each characteristic to make it an ally. Once again, people you trust can be invaluable in offering you different perspectives and suggestions.

REGULAR GUY TIP

Okay, this self-awareness thing may seem too complicated. Try this shortcut. Pick a guy you fish with who is pretty much just like you, and decide what *he should do* to be more successful. Whaada ya think? Maybe that's what *you* should do, eh?!?!

CHAPTER 4

Influential People and Events:
How *Did* You Get To Be Like This?

In the last chapter, I talked about the importance of knowing yourself. *You* are the person who has the *biggest* influence on whether or not you become a successful angler. You need to know, clearly and accurately, who that person is.

However, your professional fishing career will also benefit if you understand the important people and significant circumstances that have shaped you and your development. In my work I hear anglers recount inspirational memories of those early fishing trips with Dad or Uncle Joe, or about the supportive teacher, or attentive coach who helped keep them on the right track. Among my favorites are stories about the veteran pro angler who provided a tournament rookie with dinner and a warm motel room in place of a wet tent. I also hear tales about competitive anglers rising above criticism, proving themselves to people who said they'd never make it. Other people can support, impede, or change the course of your competitive career.

In fact, you have probably had more social and circumstantial influences in your life than you remember. The exercises that follow give you an opportunity to catalog and learn from these important people and events.

People

Let's focus on people first. In **Exercise 7,** list in the left-hand column the names of individuals who have significantly influenced your life, in either a positive or a negative way. You may find it helpful to think of your life in 10-year segments. So for example, who were the most important people in your first 10 years? How about year 10 to year 20? And so forth. Again, use friends and relatives to make sure your list is complete.

Once this list is finished, use the second and third columns to write down exactly how each person influenced you. For some people, you will only be able to make comments in one column. However, you may find there are some people who were both negative as well as positive influences.

It is hard to do this exercise quickly and still be thorough. Work on it for a bit, set it aside for awhile, and come back to it as you think of other people and how they affected you. Then look at the final column labeled Residual Influence. Write in this column the lasting impact each person has had on you.

Exercise 7: IMPORTANT PEOPLE

Name/Relationship	Positive Influences	Negative Influences	Residual Influences

A word of caution is in order here. This exercise can bring to the surface unexpected memories and emotional reactions. Over the years of using this exercise, many people have described to me vivid recollections as they wrote down and thought about those who provided assistance or inspiration. I hear comments like "You know, I had forgotten how important Mr. or Ms. Smith was to me when I was young." These are truly heartwarming moments, both for the individual, and for me!

Occasionally, however, someone will recall an unpleasant experience with a person who was a negative influence. Strong reactions, both positive and negative, are not unusual, and in most instances they will be short-lived. If you have an unpleasant reaction, put this exercise aside for a bit, or ignore it altogether. Also, if your strong emotional reactions persist, talk about them with some you trust, or seek professional assistance.

One angler who completed this exercise was effusive in describing how helpful, supportive, and instructive his Little League baseball coach had been. This same guy also told me of the critical, harsh treatment he received from his seventh-grade teacher about academic performance. It wasn't until we had been working together for some time that I realized these two people were the same person! Being able to accurately describe and come to terms with both the positive and negative characteristics of his teacher/coach allowed this angler to be more accepting of the positive and negative sides of his own temperament. As a result was he able to look at good days and bad days on the water in a more realistic light; by reacting less harshly to himself he was able to learn and improve.

So, not only will this exercise help you understand the people who have shaped your life, it will also give you some insights into the kind of people you want to affiliate with, or perhaps avoid, down the road. On many occasions, this exercise has led anglers to reconnect with people who were positive influences in days gone by. At the other end of the spectrum, I recall one particularly vivid instance where a tournament pro used the insights from this chart to stop associating with a group of people who continually brought him down.

Events

Now let's look at important events that have shaped you. Here you will list circumstances, situations, competitive events, successes, failures, and family or relationship dynamics that caused significant twists or turns.

Let me illustrate. As you know, there is fabulous fishing for many species here in my home state of Minnesota. As a youngster, my fishing pole and I were good pals. Back then, I even participated with my dad in a few multi-species fishing derbies sponsored by his company, 3M. In the Mississippi River and its backwaters we caught a little of everything, including carp, drum, mooneyes, bluegills, crappies, pike, white bass, walleyes, and sauger. However, it wasn't until I went to graduate school at the University of Missouri-St. Louis, in my mid-twenties, that the world of serious bass fishing opened up for me. My tournament bass fishing life, such as it is, and most certainly this book, might never have developed if the University of Montana had accepted me, and I had come under the influence of the fly rod/trout fishing fellas in Missoula!

Exercise 8: IMPORTANT EVENTS

Event	Positive Impact	Negative Impact	Residual Impact

Use the same basic approach as in the previous exercise. List the events, consider whether each was positive, negative, or both, and then write down the lasting influence each has had on you. This exercise can have immediate as well as long-term benefits. Once again, taking time on this exercise and using other people to make a comprehensive catalog can be an important step toward understanding the progression of your competitive career.

One top competitor I know became interested in competitive fishing because he was told over and over again that he was too small to play contact sports. I have heard this individual tell his story numerous times to many audiences. If you look closely, you can *almost always* see a glow of recognition on the faces of one or two kids in the crowd. You can also hear their internal dialogue, something like, "Yeah, that's right! You *don't* have to be 6'3" to play this game!" In this instance, a personal insight publicly revealed has become an inspiration for many.

I can't tell you exactly how this set of exercises will affect you. However, I will say that for most of you greater awareness of your unique internal and external influences will allow you to direct your fishing career the way *you* want it to go, rather than allow it be shaped or controlled by people, or past circumstances of which you are not consciously aware.

REGULAR GUY TIP

Find a cool picture of you fishing when you were a kid. Or write down a few words that describe your happiest moment fishing. Scotch tape either or both of these to your wallet, and look at them the next time you have a bad day fishing. I'm willing to bet you'll feel better.

CHAPTER 5

Catalog Your Internal Resources: What Are You Good at Now?

Since you're still reading this book, I will assume you have done the exercises in the first four chapters. You now have a sense of your commitments and how they blend with your investment in competitive angling. You also have a better understanding of yourself in relation to influential people and circumstances. You are focused on becoming a successful tournament angler. Good for you!

Here's the last step to get yourself psychologically rigged up, so to speak.

To begin with, consider this scenario: Let's say you have been talking to a Young Person (YP) for several months about the life of a competitive angler. You may have already met this kid, usually a boy, but sometimes a girl, who shows up at tournaments, asking endless questions about what it takes to be successful fishing tournaments. And let's conclude that after a while, you decide YP is committed to fishing, knows him or herself fairly well, and seems to have the drive and desire to succeed.

Before you recommend signing up for a tournament, however, you would try to help YP understand the practical side of tournament angling. You might talk to YP about boats, motors, and electronics, but you would for sure talk about rods, reels, lures, maps, and basic accessories. No sense diving into a tournament, you tell YP, until you are outfitted in a way that gives you a decent chance.

And, before you began giving advice on what equipment to get, you would ask YP to tell you about the equipment he or she already has. That is *exactly* what you will do in this chapter with your internal resources.

Before building anything, the smart person looks around to see what materials, tools, and equipment are already on hand. **Exercise 9** provides a chance to do this with the resources you have already acquired. In the business world, KSAs stands for knowledge, skills and abilities. In regular language, this represents what you know, what you have learned, and what you are currently able to do.

For example, let's say you already know how to read contour maps fairly well. Good for you. Write that down in the **Exercise 9** table. Now list other things you already know or know how to do that contribute to fishing success. Include practical skills like casting accuracy, lure selection, and boat driving. You might include competency with specific lures or techniques. Also, be sure to write down areas of knowledge, such as fish biology, seasonal movements, and baitfish patterns.

As with previous exercises, give yourself time to make your inventory complete. Don't rush through it. And again, use input from people you trust to ensure accuracy.

Exercise 9: INTERNAL RESOURCES

Internal Resources	Current Level	Ideal Level	Action Steps
Knowledge:			

Skills:	Current Level	Ideal Level	Action Steps
Abilities:	Current Level	Ideal Level	Action Steps

Once you have filled out this table, use the next two columns to grade yourself (A-, C+) for each resource, along with the grade you would like to have. In the fourth column, jot down ideas about what you could do to improve this resource from your current to your ideal level. As suggested in other chapters, think of people who could help you learn what you need to know, the ones who might teach you skills which are not currently A+.

After you have finished this exercise, take a minute and think about what you have done for yourself. Good tournament anglers do a complete tackle inventory at least once or twice a month, right? With **Exercise 9**, *and* with the information you put together about yourself in **Chapters 1-4**, you now have a comprehensive inventory of your practical *and* mental resources! You know where you are strong, you know where you need work, and you have some ideas about how to improve. Congratulate yourself! From a performance psychology perspective you are already ahead of most of the competitors on your circuit!

REGULAR GUY TIP

Ask 6 guys who have seen you fish what you are best at. If 4, 5 or all 6 of them say the same thing, believe it, and the next time fishing is really slow, go to that technique for the rest of the day. When the bite is tough, even pros fall back on what they do best!

CHAPTER 6

Keep Track:
Or Risk Getting Lost If You Don't!

The essential message in this chapter is: **Write Everything Down**. In previous chapters, there is a clear emphasis on writing, recording, and tabulating information. The reason for this is simple. There is more information for the average fisherman to keep track of than you can store in your head. Additionally, when it comes to learning new information, your memory is an inconsistent record keeper. I know, you can tell me about a specific sunken log in the back of an obscure creek in the Louisiana Delta where you caught a four pounder, and you will assert, on a stack of Bibles, that you could find that log, blindfolded, *anytime you want*! Well, that may be true! I won't argue with you about that log. At the same time, memory research clearly tells us that there are likely numerous details, some of which might be worth remembering, from that very same trip that are lost to memory. Not to worry. This chapter can help you keep track of a few more of the details that time and age erase.

So, the most obvious advantage of record keeping is that print/electronic records don't forget! Psychological research says the same thing our experience tells us, and that is that as time goes by, our recall of specific events loses precision. However, your notebook or your computer program, unlike your memory, tends to *not* spontaneously deteriorate.

Additionally, studies show that writing information down makes it easier for you to store and retrieve it. Recording enhances learning, as most of the classes you took in school demonstrated. Remember in primary school how reading and writing were closely tied together? Reading words over and over made it easier for you to learn to write them, and writing words down helped you learn to read faster. The same holds true with fishing information. Writing down important fishing data not only creates a permanent record, it also solidifies the mental pictures you have taken and the lessons you have learned!

FISHING LOG

Probably a third of the "how to" articles on tournament fishing include some reference to keeping a fishing trip log. I also strongly recommend doing this. A written record of each fishing trip will quickly turn into a personalized fishing reference book. Consider using your **Psychology of Exceptional Fishing** notebook to build a permanent record. A small amount of Internet research will also lead you to several computer programs that make it easy to collect and store fishing trip information. While you are on the water, carrying a handheld recording devise or a notebook that fits in your pocket will allow you to make immediate notes to yourself. You can later transfer these to a permanent storage system.

Whether you use an electronic version or a paper and pencil process, create an outline that includes entries for the following information:

Fishing Trip Log

Date, time, and location:

Type of water:

Species and number of fish caught:

Weather conditions:
    Wind: Temperature: Sky cover: Last 5 days:

Water conditions:
    Color: Current: Temperature: Rising/falling:

Type of cover/structure:

Lures and presentations used:

Spots/GPS coordinates:

Patterns observed:

Conclusions/lessons learned:

Things to try next time:

Try putting these headings on the inside cover of a notebook that you keep in your boat. Most fishing trips end with five, ten, or more minutes of sitting around waiting your turn to come off the lake, right? This is a perfect time to fill in your trip log. Most anglers are inclined to use this timeframe to re-sort tackle; try writing in your log instead. Tackle organization can be done in the parking lot when you are unlikely to be writing down information you don't want other anglers to see!

In addition, consider having a section in your fishing log for tournaments you observe. While you won't be able to get information from contestants *during* a tournament, once the contest is over, you can gather general data about what the winners did and approximately where they fished. You can come away from each event with a basic record of what turned out to be the winning patterns for that time of year on that body of water.

Tournament Log

If you fish tournaments, it is very important to create a special notebook just for relevant tournament information. Include here all of your fishing data, along with pertinent logistical information such as travel routes, accommodation information, and particular things to do or avoid at this tournament site.

Just last season I saw this lesson brought home to the tune of about fifteen hundred dollars. We returned to a tournament site in Northern Minnesota that had an obscure, yet solid boat ramp on the far end of the lake, and an obvious yet treacherous ramp on the near side. The guys who had written down information about ramp quality in their fishing logs saved the expensive trailer repairs that went to the one guy who didn't!

Logistical Records

In your tournament log, or elsewhere, adopt a system to keep track of phone numbers, addresses, and e-mail information for friends, relatives, emergency contacts, and certainly sponsors. The newer cell phones, PDAs and old fashioned "little black books" can all work here. Some of the best pros carry laptops with them, during practice and at tournaments, and they find a few minutes each day to catalogue important information.

Whatever system you choose, keep it handy, and use it frequently. It doesn't require much time when you are picking up tackle at a small town in Georgia to write down the name of the owner, and the name of his daughter who is about to graduate from high school. However, I can tell you from experience that by storing and using that information you will likely receive a warm reception when you call in advance of next year's tournament to find out if they have a good supply of the Double-Bladed Supersonic Gully Whompers that won the tournament last time!

Filing Systems

Any good filing system can work—you may decide to keep track of information by lake type, by season of the year, or by state or region. The best computer programs allow you to access data using any of these key search words. And as suggested, a small notebook or a pocket tape recorder you carry with you in your boat can be invaluable, especially on days when you are practicing or exploring. It's worth restating; you can only store so many details in your head. If you use practical recording tools, you *will* have an edge on the competition!

When I first started tournament fishing, I watched Loel and his partner come to the scales with ten fish that weighed over thirty-five pounds! Afterwards in the parking lot we stood around next to a large cooler and talked about what happened. After everybody left, I wrote down a few notes. By the time next season rolled around, my *recollection* was they caught their fish on jigs in the reeds. The trouble was, when I returned to check out this pattern, reed beds covered about a third of that particular lake. Nevertheless, whenever I was in the area, I stopped, and with high hopes tried to reproduce their success. I did not.

Some years later, our club decided to hold a tournament on that lake. I dutifully went back and looked up my notes, and this time I read the fine print. There, in my own handwriting, were the words "reeds with cane together." With that precise information in hand, my co-angler and I finished first and second. It was my record, not my memory, which made all the difference!

Just like lures are tools, so too, are recording devises. And it may seem tedious at times to put all this effort into record keeping. Additionally, it may not be obvious that top professional anglers do this. Let me tell you a secret: They Do!

REGULAR GUY TIP

For about five or ten bucks you can get a pocket-size calendar that you want to put in your tackle box. Then, whenever you think of it, write down on the correct date, the number of fish you caught and where you got 'em. At the end of the year, see if your calendar doesn't remember things you forgot. Then maybe *next year* you'll make a **real** fishing log!

CHAPTER 7

You *Can* Get There from Here:
How to Set Attainable Goals!

When it comes to improving performance, few techniques are as consistently effective as goal-setting. This chapter will explain what goal-setting can do for you, and illustrate ways to create effective long-range, short-term, and immediate goals. Traditionally, people set goals just after Christmas. They're called New Year's Resolutions. However, as is painfully obvious, those goals rarely work as planned. It is said that "The road to Hell is paved with good intentions." If that's true then that pavement is most certainly resurfaced every January!

The problem with most goals is that they are not well-designed. Bargain-basement tackle stores have colorful racks of spinnerbaits that look like lit-up Christmas trees. They sell for a $1.99. However, serious fishermen pass by these attractive displays in favor of spinnerbaits with top-shelf components such as premium blades, ball-bearing swivels, and chemically sharpened hooks. You want your goals to be of similar quality.

How Goals Work

Decades of psychological research show that effective goals do several things. Most obviously, higher goals lead to higher expectations, which in turn lead to better performance. Conventional wisdom says the same thing: you often get what you expect to get. (Not always, of course, but often enough to have it matter!) If you set modest goals and expect medium-level performance, that is more than likely what will happen. If you set your sights high, then expectations will rise, and performance will tend to follow along.

Goals also direct your attention and effort toward positive outcomes. For example, having a goal to determine how different jig-and-trailer combinations come through various types of cover will focus your attention on the specifics of head design, hook style, weedguard configuration, and trailer shape and composition that you might not otherwise have noticed.

35

Perhaps even more importantly, goals concentrate your effort in ways that tune out distractions. If your goal is to place a specific cast in a precise spot, you can become so intently focused that you end up essentially oblivious to potential frustrations such as rough water, or the irritating sounds of jet skiers!

Creating goals also tends to boost your energy and enthusiasm. This is one of those areas where professional fishermen can learn from laboratory rats. A rat wandering in a maze without a clear objective looks a lot like a tournament fisherman listlessly casting about in a large cove with no specific objective in mind. However, when that lab rat figures out there is a certain path to follow that has a piece of cheese at the end, his energy and activity levels increase significantly. Likewise, the competitive fisherman in the cove will be much more energized and enthused about positioning his boat and presenting his bait in a precise manner if he has a particular goal or set of goals to pursue.

Goals also positively affect persistence. Having a list of goals that includes covering secondary points with crankbaits, exploring flats with rattle baits, and flipping rock walls with tubes will help you persevere until you accomplish each of these objectives.

Goals and Forward Thinking

It may not be immediately obvious, but here is one more benefit to goal-setting. In many instances, setting specific goals leads to a chain of complex thoughts and plans that help your goals become reality. Several research studies show that when engaging in complex tasks (like tournament fishing!) individuals automatically begin thinking and problem solving when presented with challenging goals.

Prove this to yourself by focusing on the goal of, say, driving to your next tournament. Think about that spot for a couple of minutes and see what happens. Okay, now stop and consider what your mind just did. Perhaps some of you started thinking about the route you would travel to this tournament. With no conscious effort, you began creating a travel plan in your mind. Pretty cool, huh? Alternately, you may have wandered in your mind from the specifics of the lake to the likely seasonal patterns that may apply during this event, and perhaps you began mentally assembling a list of baits and presentations you will need to take with you to that tournament. Without much effort, that complex information-processing center on your shoulders spontaneously began creating plans and started

36

putting steps in place once you had envisioned your goal!

How to Create Goals

Now let's do some actual goal-setting. Use your **Psychology of Exceptional Fishing** notebook, or the chart in **Exercise 10** to structure this process. To begin with, you need three separate time frames for goals: Long-range, short-term, and immediate. Start with long-range goals. These are your dreams and aspirations. For the sake of illustration, let's say you want to win your local Tournament of Champions (TOC) event sometime within the next 5 years. Great! Write this down in the long-range goals section. And don't be afraid to think big. When it comes to long-range goals, don't sell yourself short. Once you commit to this goal, think about it for a few days and see if it's something you really want to do. If it is, go out on a limb and tell some of your fishing buddies and a few of your close friends about your long-term goal. Research studies definitely indicate that a public commitment to goals enhances your commitment to them.

Next you will need short term goals. To extend the previous example, in order to win the tournament of champions event, you may have to qualify for it, and this will lead to a series of medium-range objectives for the tournaments leading up to next year's TOC. In your notebook, write down monthly goals between now and the end of the year. As you create each of these goals, make them as specific as possible. Also, use precise time frames whenever possible. For example, creating a pre-spawn tournament goal to catch fish on both jerkbaits and soft plastics will be more effective than a general goal of trying to do your best in the spring.

Now focus on your immediate goals. These will need your attention for a few minutes every week or two until the TOC. See if you can find something to do every day, or at least a few things each week to move you closer to your long-range goal. If you do, you will be more likely to realize your goal than if you wait until the day before each tournament.

Pre-rigging rods is a great example of an effective immediate goal. You already know how much more likely you are to experiment with a bait you already have tied on than you are to stop in the middle of a practice or tournament day and assemble a new rod/reel/lure configuration.

Exercise 10:   GOAL-SETTING

Long Range Goals
1)
2)
3)

Short Term Goals
1)
2)
3)
4)
5)
6)
7)
8)
9)

Immediate Goals
1)
2)
3)
4)
5)
6)
7)
8)
9)

Feedback

Lack of specific, accurate feedback causes more goals to fail than all other reasons combined! You can have the most detailed, specific, well-organized set of goals imaginable, yet without accurate information to tell you whether or not you are closing in on your objectives, you might as well be in the middle of Okeechobee in the fog!

It is very important to set up regular check points to evaluate your progress against your goals. As you write down long-range, short-term, and immediate goals, include target dates to evaluate your progress. Then, you can either recommit to your present goals or create new ones.

Motivation

In some instances, people lose motivation and wind up feeling deflated if their goals do not quickly become reality. Often times, the problem is that the goals themselves are unrealistic. In order for goals to work, you have to get after them and stay after them, at least for a reasonable amount of time. However, staying motivated to pursue *unrealistic* goals is quite difficult. Psychology research tells us that motivation is a function of the attractiveness of the goal *and* the perceived probability of success. In regular language that means the goal has to be something you want, and it has to be something *you believe* you have a reasonable chance of obtaining. A goal like someday winning the *FLW Tour Championship* can be energizing and motivating, though if your goal is to do that this year you may end up frustrated, disappointed, and inclined to give up.

As mentioned, when it comes to long-range goals, feel free to think big. Let your heart, your dreams, and your spirit override the practical side of your brain when envisioning long-range goals.

However, at least with short-term and immediate goals, try to maintain some sense of realism. Remember, wildly unrealistic expectations eventually create tension. If you came in dead last in your club last year, you will most likely experience frustration and tension if your short-term goal is to win every tournament this year! Goals that stretch us beyond what we normally would accomplish can lead to optimal performance. The phenomenon of being "In the Zone" that you will read about in **Chapter 17** reflects this process of using difficult yet obtainable goals to enhance performance. Unobtainable, unrealistic goals cause frustration and hopelessness, however.

Decades of psychological research tell us this: goal-setting works. As a new season unfolds, your goals will guide, motivate, and inspire you in ways you have yet to realize!

REGULAR GUY TIP

So maybe setting all kinds of goals seems like a lot of work. It doesn't have to be. Just flip back a couple pages and write some stuff down for the long-range, short-term, immediate goals. It'll take less than five minutes. Isn't better fishing worth five more minutes?

CHAPTER 8

Create a Positive Mental Framework:
Some Assembly Required!

What's more satisfying than a fishing day when you "absolutely know" you are going to catch nice fish? Sure, it's fun to catch a big one, and doing well in competition is great. And of course winning tournaments is *very* rewarding. However, I bet your experience matches mine (and the stories I hear from countless anglers) that nothing really beats that feeling you have when your heart, head, and soul are in alignment, the days when you leave the ramp in the morning with the rock-solid belief that "Yep, today we are *gonna get 'em*!"

And wouldn't it be great if you could put yourselves in that kind of positive mental framework on a regular basis? Well, this chapter will help move you in that direction!

To begin with, let's take a look at what's going on internally and externally on those "perfect days." To begin with, the days where you know you are going to catch them typically start with a clear, unequivocal sense of where the fish are and what you are going to do. In most instances, you've done your homework, maybe you've talked to some other anglers, and perhaps you've even done some pre-fishing. In any case, you have a solid plan. In addition, you likely have a back-up plan, and maybe even backup plans for your backup plan! Clearly you are well-prepared in terms of what, when, where, and how the day will unfold.

At the same time, you have unquestioning confidence in all of your equipment, down to the specific size and color of the lures that are sure to work. (You also have second, third, and fourth lure options in mind!)

On the flip side, those perfect days also include a clear absence of anxiety, worry, apprehension, and frustration. Your calm, confident optimism essentially eliminates *any* disruptive thoughts or distressful emotions.

Sometimes those perfect days result in good fish right away. Your first lure choice and first spot click, and Bang!......your magic day has begun!

Other perfect days start out slower, though you maintain a relaxed, seamless belief that today is going to be a good day. One of my favorite stories in this vein is about a seasoned angler (Joe) who had been trying for years to get his good buddy (T.A.) from out of town to fish Secret Lake with him. Finally, the day arrived, and a perfect day it was: calm, mild, stable weather, relatively little boat traffic; in short, primo mid-summer conditions. Joe knew *exactly* where the fish would be! Except the fish *weren't* there! At least they weren't on the first spot. Or the second spot. Or the third or fourth spots! Places that had held large concentrations of big fish in years past produced nary a bite.

As Joe told me the story, he had come to the lake that morning with that rare, relaxed confidence we all envy and seek, and he knew, *he just flat knew,* the fish would bite once he found them. Hours later, on the *ninth spot* they tried, Joe and T.A. finally came across the Mother Lode. In Joe's words, they just "wore 'em out" for the better part of an hour. "Other days" Joe said, "I would have panicked, got nervous, and started frantically running around lake. But on this day, for some reason, *I knew* we'd get 'em. And we did!"

However, it seems as though some days you have that calm, confident feeling, whereas most days you do not. Let's look at what Performance Psychology tells us can be done to make those good days more frequent.

Being consistent in your fishing performance is what you want, right? How about if you create mental consistency first, and see if fishing consistency doesn't follow? It just makes sense that if you can consistently "get your mind right" you will be far ahead of your peers, eh? Consider the concept of consistency in terms of controllable and uncontrollable variables. Creating a positive mental framework involves understanding controllable and uncontrollable variables, and finding adaptive psychological ways to deal with both.

For this exercise, use your **Psychology of Exceptional Fishing** notebook or the tables below to get a handle on how you deal with controllable and uncontrollable variables.

Controllable Variables

On the controllable variables page, make a comprehensive list of all the physical equipment and physical preparation dimensions you regularly face. Be as specific as possible here. Rods, tackle, equipment, and logistical planning items go in this column. Also include a section on tournament knowledge. Tracking your own results, as well as the results of other tournaments on the bodies of water you regularly fish could be on this list. Understanding fish patterns in various water systems during different seasons also represents a set of controllable variables.

You should also list major psychological dimensions. Attitude, your capacity to pay attention, and the ability to deal with stress are among the many mental variables over which you have at least some control.

Once this list is done, use the second column to write down how you typically react when each variable goes wrong. Let's use your outboard motor as one controllable variable. As these tables indicate, there is a space for you to comment on your typical Emotional Response when this variable gets goofed up (E-R? Angry, frustrated, annoyed?), as well as a space for you to write down your typical Practical Response (P-R? Quit, give up, try again, get help?).

Here again, honesty with yourself will allow you to understand which controllable variables typically cause the most difficulty. To illustrate, some tournament pros wait until the last minute to make housing plans for upcoming tournaments. If this controllable variable causes you difficulty, use this awareness (and your calendar!) to eliminate this potential source of worry and apprehension. You may not find many controllable variables that are disruptive. It would be worth doing this exercise just to find that out, don't you think?

Uncontrollable Variables

Pros find this exercise extremely valuable. On the uncontrollable variables chart, make an equally comprehensive list. Obvious uncontrollable variables are things like weather, water level, and available cover. Include also things like disruptive spectator boats, personality clashes with sponsors, and lousy food at Frank's Bar and Grill in Frostbite Falls, Minnesota.

This list is fun to talk over with fellow competitors. You may have fun telling "what went wrong" stories to each other as you make your lists complete. Once you have finished, write down your emotional and practical response to each of these variables.

Exercise 11:

CONTROLLABLE & UNCONTROLLABLE VARIABLES

Controllable Variable	Emotional Response Practical Response
	E-R? P-R?
	E-R? P-R?
	E-R? P-R?
	E-R? P-R?
	E-R? P-R?
	E-R? P-R?
	E-R? P-R?
	E-R? P-R?
	E-R? P-R?
	E-R? P-R?
	E-R? P-R?
	E-R? P-R?
	E-R? P-R?
	E-R? P-R?
	E-R? P-R?
	E-R? P-R?

Uncontrollable Variables	Emotional Response Practical Response
	E-R? P-R?
	E-R? P-R?
	E-R? P-R?
	E-R? P-R?
	E-R? P-R?
	E-R? P-R?
	E-R? P-R?
	E-R? P-R?
	E-R? P-R?
	E-R? P-R?
	E-R? P-R?
	E-R? P-R?
	E-R? P-R?
	E-R? P-R?
	E-R? P-R?

You don't have to show these lists to anyone, so be candid with yourself. If spectators get too close and really tick you off, and you don't have a particularly good strategy for tuning them out or asking them to back off, write that down. Openly acknowledging the variables that cause you difficulty will provide an opportunity to explore them, and also experiment with new and potentially more adaptive responses.

I can't tell you how many times I have had anglers do this exercise and then call me up and say "Hey, I never thought of what I usually do in that situation." Well, okay, you have a chance to think about it now! The point is, you don't really want to wait until you run into an uncontrollable variable on the road or on the water and then have to figure out what to do on the spot. You can't expect yourself to be as efficient or as comprehensive when thinking on the fly as when you can spend time considering your options in advance. With forethought and consultation from your pals at least two or three choices for each situation will likely come up for the next time you encounter these uncontrollable variables!

A young pro I worked with identified "Someone beats me to my first spot" as a recurrent, bothersome uncontrollable variable. All he could say about this variable was that it made him very angry. He couldn't think of a single practical response to effectively handle this situation. After discussing this issue with several people, he came to realize he often wasted somewhere between 30 and 60 minutes fuming and sputtering before he was able to calm down, refocus, and get back to fishing.

Needless to say, this was a valuable discovery for Mr. Up-and-Coming Tournament Pro. Once he saw he was wasting substantial segments of his fishing day, he became open to other options. He learned and practiced refocusing exercises, I showed him some negotiating strategies, and we talked through ways he could use his good planning skills to shift from spot A to spot B quickly and less emotionally. And while he has not yet won the Angler of the Year award in his club, he has reported that he rarely throws away fishing time on temper tantrums any more.

Having numerous strategies for coping with controllable and uncontrollable variables is like having several lures in your tackle box for deep water, for shallow ledges, or for submerged trees. The more tactics/lures you have at your disposal, the more control you will have over your mental framework, and ultimately the more "We're-gonna-get-'em-today-for-sure" days you will have!

REGULAR GUY TIP

Pick out *the* most upsetting situation you encountered last year. Ask three good fishing buddies *who weren't there at the time* how they would have handled the situation. At least *one* of them will have a better idea of what to do than what you did. Guaranteed!

CHAPTER 9

Use Routines and Rituals:
It Ain't Just The Shirt, *But* The Shirt Helps!

In the last chapter, you read about the importance of cataloguing controllable and uncontrollable variables. In this chapter, you will learn the advantages and disadvantages of using structured routines and systems to make your time on the water more efficient.

Fishing is a complex sport. Regardless of how and where you fish, you regularly deal with lots of variables and tons of information, and it all seems to matter! Trying to catch finny critters appears to require an arsenal of complex equipment, a full understanding of weather and water conditions, and an aquatic biologist's knowledge of fish behavior and migration patterns. To the casual observer, this may seem to be more information than anyone could possibly comprehend, leading to the false conclusion that fishing is a chaotic pastime in which pure luck, not skill, plays the biggest part.

However, I'd say you're probably a pretty savvy angler, and able to recognize the difference between important and unimportant information. If you are, then you're in perfect position to use Routines and Rituals to bring order, stability, and predictability to the important fishing variables. How? Keep reading!

Practical Routines

From a practical perspective, many of the controllable variables listed on your worksheet in **Chapter 8** can best be handled by the use of structured routines and checklists. You probably already have routine boat and tow vehicle maintenance schedules. You may also have regularly scheduled routines for inspecting and repairing rods, reels, and terminal tackle. (If you don't, you should!) Most importantly, you need a pre-trip routine, one that allows time for charging batteries, filling fuel tanks, and assembling additional equipment like life jackets that actually fit the people in your boat.

A few years ago at a seminar on this topic, a young professional angler in the crowd talked about his pre-tournament routine, and during the question-and-answer session he showed his checklist to the audience. I made what at the time seemed like a throwaway comment, something to the effect of, "A similar checklist would be good for tournaments. Then on the back you could create a different routine/checklist for fishing with kids or friends." The pro angler later told me he nodded and agreed that was a good idea. I don't remember that.

What I do remember is this guy calling me about six weeks later, telling me in an excited voice that his checklist probably saved someone's life. Turns out he went back to his motel room the night of our seminar and did what we had discussed, making a new routine/checklist for fishing in non-tournament settings. Somewhere on the list he put this item: Check to make sure each person's life jacket fits snugly. On the day he called me, the 3 year-old daughter of one of his best friends had fallen overboard. "Everyone went crazy", he told me. "We were all in panic mode for several minutes, screaming, pleading, trying to get the boat turned around to pick Melissa up. It all turned out fine, but it was the list, man, it was that list! If I hadn't checked and adjusted her life jacket, she could have easily slid right out of it and drowned."

So, maybe your list of routine things won't have such a dramatic effect. Maybe you'll just save yourself the inconvenience of having to go back home to retrieve essential equipment you forgot. Or, perhaps your routine checklist will save you the pain and expense of unnecessary repairs. Routines, however, especially those that are written down, increase the likelihood that you'll remember *all* of the important things you need to have and do when you go fishing.

Also, create a routine and a checklist for the end of each trip. Have you ever seen someone's boat sitting in the middle of the road because the guy was in a hurry and forgot to secure all the tie-downs straps? I have, and it's not a pretty scene. It only takes a few minutes to walk around your boat with your checklist before you drive off; however, the headaches and money you save may be substantial.

Tournament Routines

As a competitive angler, routines and checklists will address the numerous controllable variables that go into preparing for tournaments, including managing relationships with sponsors. Like my seminar colleague, most competitive anglers save time, effort, and money by routinely using checklists for tournament preparation. You may already do this yourself. If you don't, use your **Psychology of Exceptional Fishing** notebook to make a list of the several things you need to consider prior to a tournament. See if you can divide your list into tasks that can be done a month in advance, those that can be done a week ahead of time, and those to be taken care of on tournament day or the night before.

Consider using a similar checklist for communicating with your sponsors. For those of us who are introverts, this will be especially helpful, as we tend to wait for others to call us rather than pick up the phone or use e-mail to check in as often as we should. Use a day planner, calendars, or a computer to maintain regular communication with sponsor contacts.

A scheduled routine for the twenty-four hours prior to a tournament can be especially helpful. Many professional anglers have successfully used a pre-tournament routine to take care of as many practical dimensions as possible the day or night before a tournament. One pro who did this exercise told me he made the rather simple decision to fill his truck and boat with gasoline as soon as he got off the water rather than leave this potentially time-consuming detail for the morning. As much as this saved him time, it also saved him the mental anguish of wondering which gas stations would be open early, how far out of his way he would have to drive to get gas, and so forth. The goal here is to avoid the common experience of sitting in your boat before take-off thinking about the preparations you should have done but didn't. Fill the time before fishing with confidence; leave doubt and worry on the dock! A pre-trip routine can help you do this!

Mental Routines

In **Chapter 19** I will describe in greater detail how to assemble a personalized package of mental techniques that will become your **Psychological Tackle Box**. Let me introduce now the idea that mental routines are vitally important all by themselves. They also help you get the most out of the performance psychology tactics you adopt. Top competitors in most sports use specific psychological routines prior to and during events. Do you? Take a moment to ask yourself: how routinely do you check and sharpen hooks? Check knots and retie lures? Replace line? Visit the fish in your livewell? Check and set the drag or spool tension on your reels? These are just some of the areas where mental routines can clearly make a significant positive difference.

But, maybe you think mental routines don't make that much difference. If you knew Michael Anti, you would think differently. At the 2004 Summer Olympics in Athens, Mr. Anti won the silver medal in the 50 M Free Rifle shooting event. In the final round, each competitor took 120 shots, and with one shot to go Mr. Anti was so far ahead of the next competitor his last shot did not need to be perfect, it only needed to hit his target *somewhere*. It did not! Mr. Anti later admitted in interviews that what happened was he failed to go through his entire mental routine before his last shot. And so, when he pulled the trigger, he hit the target next to his. He lost the gold medal by 8/10 of a point!

Rituals

Many successful athletes use songs, meditation, prayer, and other contemplative rituals in preparation for competitive events. Each of you must explore your own path in this domain; however, research clearly indicates what you may intuitively know, that people who engage in religious or spiritual rituals tend to be psychologically better off than those who do not. Contemplative, meditative, religious practices are associated with improved concentration, diminished anxiety, and greater self-assurance, these dimensions also being positively linked to peak performance. Reading, personal reflection, and discussions with friends or family may help you find rituals that work for you.

In addition, you might find value in mundane rituals such as what you eat the night before a tournament, or what you carry to the dock on tournament morning. Numerous professional athletes use such rituals. Historically, clothing has had ritualistic meaning in competitive events. Professionals in several sports are quite particular about what they wear, and how they get dressed on game day. So if you have a favorite hat or jacket you prefer, wear it with pride, knowing you are part of a long tradition. Just remember, it ain't just the shirt!

Superstitious Behavior

Not all routine behavior is psychologically healthy, however. In extreme form, systems, schedules, and rituals can result in a narrow, constricted outlook, and rigid, unimaginative, or perhaps magical thinking. Athletes seem especially susceptible to overusing rituals and routines. Individuals can become quite distraught if their favorite routines are disrupted. For example, you probably have heard stories about professional athletes who put on their uniforms in exactly the same sequence, and who had to undress and start over if they mistakenly put on something out of sequence. Other competitors destroy equipment or burn clothing after a poor performance. To most people, this represents ritualized behavior that has gone too far.

Fishing author John Geirach wrote "Beliefs can make data invisible", and so it is for people who overestimate the value of particular behavior rituals or unique routines. It may be difficult for you to recognize when routines that may have worked in the past have become extreme and no longer useful. Trust your friends, family, and fellow competitors here. If more than a few people question one of your routines, you would do well to examine and reconsider it.

For the most part, however, routines can help decrease ambiguity and uncertainty, eliminate unnecessary decisions, and allow us to concentrate our energies on the immediate issues of finding and catching fish. Try adding a more systematic, routine approach to the predictable aspects of fishing and watch your efficiency improve!

REGULAR GUY TIP

The one routine you *absolutely* need is for boat and trailer maintenance. Ask a marine mechanic you trust how often you should get your motor tuned up and your trailer serviced. Then do what he says. Just do it! You probably have a neighbor or a cousin who never got around to changing the oil on his car or truck, and eventually he blew the engine. Since you're smart enough to not do *that*, be smart enough to regularly service your boat and trailer!

CHAPTER 10

Time Management:
Make Notebooks and Calendars Your Friends!

One of the trickiest performance psychology dimensions to master is time management. When you think about setting goals, dealing with controllable and uncontrollable variables, or creating practical plans and routines, you probably don't often consider the significance of time management. However, experience and psychological research both tell us this is a mistake. Have you ever vigorously attacked a list of activities only to end up leaving something important unfinished because you ran out of time? Of course you have; so have the rest of us. This chapter will keep that from happening too often!

The primary tenet of time management is "**Manage Your Time, Not the Work**." What does that mean? Well, for starters it means there are always more things to do than there is time to do them in; but you *knew that!* Think of managing time as equivalent to managing money. When you walk into a bait shop, for example, there are always more lures you *want to buy* than you have money for in your wallet. The smart shopper (that would be you!) will make careful decisions about how to spend the money you have, rather than just throw lures in your shopping cart, regardless of how much they cost! Managing time effectively turns on the same principle: since you never have too much time, you need to make smart decisions about how you spend the time you have.

You probably know people who take time on Sunday afternoon or evening to make a list of what they need to do in the week ahead. Perhaps you do this. Or maybe you're the type who plans tomorrow today; if so, you may sit down each evening to think about, or write down what needs to happen the next day. However, when tomorrow arrives, you may be pleasantly, or perhaps unpleasantly surprised by situations or circumstances you need to handle that aren't on your list!

"That's life", you say. True enough. If you were planning to work on your fishing tackle, for example, and your daughter's ride to soccer practice falls through, you are likely to set your tackle aside and attend to what Ms. Missy needs. However, that doesn't mean you should abandon your initial list or plan.

Put First Things First

One of the best self-help books ever written is called *The Seven Habits of Highly Effective People* by Stephen Covey. If you haven't read this book, you should. It is practical, down to earth, and filled with lots of concrete suggestions about how to be more effective, both personally and professionally. Mr. Covey also has a leadership foundation that has created seminars built around each of his seven habits, one of which is called *Put First Things First*. I have heard from people who know that the *Put First Things First* seminar is requested by businesses, organizations, and church groups more often than all of the other habit-related seminars put together! Managing time, setting priorities, and sticking with things that matter are universally challenging, it appears!

If you're like most people, even when you make to-do lists, you probably go after the smallest and easiest things first, in order to get them out of the way. Alternately, you may quickly skim your list and start with whatever seems like it needs to get done immediately. Mr. Covey suggests, and I agree, that before you move into action it helps to prioritize your daily or weekly lists. This means looking at your list and asking yourself: "Which of the things on my list, if completed now, would give me the most benefit?" Alternately, you could ask yourself "Which item, if left unattended (for a day, a week) would cause me the biggest headache?" (You could also be extremely thorough and rank all the items on your to-do list in order of importance!)

Obviously, you don't always have to do things *exactly* in sequence, the most important thing first, next most important item second, etc. Nevertheless, writing down what is important and what is not will keep things that matter at the top of your list until they get done! Just as importantly, prioritizing your list decreases the likelihood that you will spend precious time on tasks of minimal value.

One pro gave me an interesting framework for the prioritizing part of time management. He told me that when he looks through his list of activities he tries to identify the ones that resemble trailer bearings. Curious, I asked him what he meant. He graciously explained. "You know, trailer bearings are invisible. By themselves, they don't get your attention until something goes wrong. Still, they are vitally important, and even though you can't see them, they need attention on a regular basis. So, when I go over my lists, I pick out the things that look like trailer bearings, and I do those things first."

Once you have decided *what* tasks are important, you can use calendars or day planners to decide *when* you will take care of them. Office-supply centers, drugstores, and places like Target have such tools to list and track activities. It is a truism that if an action item is on your calendar, it gets done; if its not, then it doesn't.

Some of us detail freaks can end up spending an inordinate amount of time making lists, checking and rechecking calendars, and prioritizing and reprioritizing our activities. Obviously, you want to use lists, calendars, and planners as tools to help you; you don't want them to become burdensome. However, my 30 years of clinical work have led me to the same conclusion Mr. Covey presents in his book, and that is this: very few people spend enough time on planning, prioritizing and time management.

So, keep Mr. Covey's *Put First Things First* concept in mind when making and carrying out plans, lists, and timelines. And see if you can't find a way to use that fishy *Bass Pro Shops* calendar you got for Christmas! You'll be glad you did.

Nevertheless....................

Distractions Require Reprioritization

No matter how good your plans are, or how clear your priorities appear to be, you *will get distracted* and be thrown off course now and again. For example, let's say you have set aside two hours to do your tackle, when all of a sudden your cell phone rings and a sponsor, or Uncle Bob wants to talk. The next thirty minutes race by pretty fast, and now you only have an hour and a half to do a two hour job.

Here is where the *Put First Things First* principle becomes particularly valuable. Facing the scenario described above, start by telling yourself that you weren't going to get all your tackle done in the first place. Now, instead of a two-hour tackle session, you have a ninety-minute window; you need to re-decide what the most important pieces of tackle are to work on, and which ones you can let go until later.

Use this same principle to manage your time on the water, either during practice or on tournament days. Uncontrollable variables like rough water, fog delays, and spectator boats can unexpectedly interfere with your fishing plans. You may also *occasionally* spend more time on one spot or with one bait than you intended! Suddenly, you realize with dismay that your day is half over! A common response in this situation is to become apprehensive and/or distraught. Internal dialogues go something like this: "Aw, &*%&$*&! ....I've just wasted four hours! Now I won't be able to get to all my spots!" If your anxiety builds too much, or if panic takes over, you can wind up spinning your wheels intellectually and emotionally, and waste even more time! Sound familiar? Well, don't give up. There's hope!

Competitive anglers with good time management skills will stop at that point and try to calmly reassess the situation. An adaptive internal dialogue might go something like this: "I started the day with an eight hour tournament. Now I'm looking at a four hour tournament. What would be the best way to use my time in a four hour tournament? What is my next best spot? And what spots do I want to make sure I hit before my four hours are up?"

Once again, the focus is on managing your time rather than the activity or the event itself. You almost always have control over what you do with your time. However, you don't always over have control over the circumstances you encounter. Resolve to make daily/weekly lists, address the most important things first, and when distractions occur simply review your checklist and recommit to doing the next most important thing next!

REGULAR GUY TIP

Ask yourself and two fishing pals what *one thing* you most often forget when you go fishing. Write that down on a piece of paper and tape it to your tackle box where you can see it. At the end of the season, you will have forgotten that particular thing less often. That *should* convince you to do a more comprehensive list next year!

CHAPTER 11

Get Feedback and Revise:
That's Not *Exactly* It, But You're Close!

No question, tournament angling is real athletic competition. The essence of sport is skill, and clearly the most skilled anglers prevail most of the time. While there are individual differences in natural fishing talent, there are also, regrettably, wide differences in dedication to practice and improvement. Remember that person in high school who made the team just because he or she was a fabulous natural athlete? People like that didn't do extra practice, they didn't go to the weight room very often, and they certainly didn't push themselves as hard as some of us did. They just showed up, with enough innate talent to play well without doing much work. The world of competitive fishing also contains such individuals. However, this is *not* the kind of competitor you want to be. Rather, these are the people you should strive to pass on the leaderboard in tournaments. And you can, if you make a commitment to practice and improve!

Practice Fishing

Practice fishing, for most competitive anglers, means going to the lake and using the skills and techniques they already have to locate fish prior to a tournament. However, that is a far cry from what practice looks like in other sports. No reasonable basketball coach, for example, would spend the three days prior to a game just scrimmaging. But that is essentially what tournament fishermen do. Similarly, if you went to your son's or daughter's soccer camp and all the coach did was divide players up into dark shirts and white shirts and let them play, you would blow a fuse!

And rightly so! You recognize, at least for other sports, that just playing the game is not an efficient way to *learn and improve*. Basketball, soccer, football, and baseball players practice a wide range of specific offensive and defensive skills. Athletes at all levels perform drills, run plays over and over again, and try variations of different techniques to see what works best. For example, a good basketball player should be able to dribble with both hands. If you are right-handed you may recall the frustrations of practicing your left-hand dribble. However, when you finally got it, and then executed a crossover dribble in a game, blowing by some surprised opponent on his offside…well, that was a great day. But is that what you do when practice fishing? I am willing to bet it is not. When I bring this up to anglers they tell me that those three days prior to a tournament is not the right time to be experimenting with new techniques. Okay, I'll buy that. But do you have other time set aside during the year for specific skill development? I'm suggesting you should.

A world champion angler told me that one of the best pieces of advice he ever received was to learn to cast with both hands. You might think this is not a big deal. Casting with your non-dominant hand won't make much of a difference during the course of a season, you might say. That opinion, and others like it, could be worth reconsidering. And here are two reasons why. Like many of you, I fish Pro-Am tournaments from the back of the boat. Because of where I stand, and because I am right-handed, I have had to learn to cast accurately with my left hand. When a right-handed pro is on a dock pattern, for example, my right hand cast is useless. On more than a few occasions, I have watched pros pull away from dock fish they missed because they could not throw back to them with a left-handed presentation. In one particular instance, I caught a three pounder that my right-handed pro left behind. So what, you ask? Well, in that particular event my pro came in second by four ounces!

Additionally, some pro anglers have been diagnosed with casting-related Repetitive Motion Injury that required surgery. Will casting with both hands prevent this? I can't offer an opinion, though it might be wise to hear what your local sport medicine physician has to say on this topic.

Individual Skill Development

Alright, so maybe casting with both hands doesn't interest you. However, in reviewing your tournament performance from last year and setting goals for this year, I strongly encourage building into your schedule dedicated time for individual skill development. In previous chapters, you catalogued your strengths and weaknesses. At least on an annual basis, you should update this list. Top competitors in all sports do.

Whether it's deep cranks, drop shots, or spoon fishing, you should pick two or three specific techniques in which you are not currently solid and build a practice schedule to increase your proficiency. Consider also peripheral dimensions like learning more about your electronics.

Seriously, how many of those six zillion features on your state-of-the-art LCD menu do you truly understand how to use?

I know, it can be boring going out on a lake and just working on one technique, say drop shotting, for an extended period of time. It can be especially difficult to keep at it when you know there is a great topwater bite up near shore! However, go back to the left-hand dribble. You didn't learn that in five minutes, or in one day, did you? There were plenty of times in the driveway at home when you kept practicing instead of taking off with your buddies. Consider using that same attitude here.

Or think of it this way: how many tournaments (or just regular fishing trips!) did you have last year where one more good fish would have made a difference? So, are you willing to work hard and do real practice, or are you just going to scrimmage again this year?

Break It Down

Once you have chosen an area you want to improve, take a few minutes to consider the different components of the technique you want to master. Let's say you picked improving your effectiveness with deep crankbaits. Articles, crankbait experts, videotapes, the internet, and weekend fishing shows like **Bass Edge** can explain and show good rod, reel, and line setups. But what about your crankbait assortment? Do you have enough sizes and models of crankbaits to cover the part of the water column you want to fish? If you're not sure, use the information sources listed above to find out. As you assemble information, use your **Psychology of Exceptional Fishing** notebook to write down what you learn.

Next comes the challenging part. Go to the lake with your notebook and your crankbait equipment and commit to spending 20-30 minutes with it. Don't try to force yourself to stay with deep cranks all day (there's that topwater bite, remember!?) You want learning to be fun. So make your first experiment-and-practice session short, and then set up another practice time fairly soon. Research shows that learning spread over several sessions is better than cramming new information in all at once!

On this practice dimension, it doesn't matter if you fish competitively or not. If you want to fish better than you did last year, you need to practice new skills. If you do fish tournaments, your circuit is no different than the *Bassmaster Elite Series* or the *FLW Tour*. Every year, young anglers who are willing to work hard and practice long hours are finishing ahead of veterans with more experience and knowledge. In competitive fishing, as in every other sport, if you are not seriously practicing and getting better, you are probably falling behind.

Obtaining Accurate Feedback

Once you make a commitment to improve, you must find a way to get accurate feedback. The importance of obtaining accurate feedback is another area where psychological research and common sense say exactly the same thing. In order to be good, you have to see, hear, or otherwise perceive how your performance stacks up against some type of standard. Going back to the basketball player, it is vitally important to see how close the ball is to the basket in order for the hoopster to adjust his/her shot. Alternately, musicians need to hear the notes they are playing in order to make corrections in pitch. Top performers everywhere need specific, immediate feedback.

Competitive as well as noncompetitive fishermen also need feedback to become experts in their craft. However, you rarely have access to immediate feedback in the same way other performers do. With the exception of sight fishing, seldom is there direct evidence of how close your bait is to a fish, or whether a particular retrieve interested or repulsed your prey. You could be off by a fraction of an inch, or you could be on the wrong side of the lake altogether. In most cases it's impossible to tell.

Which is why being a successful tournament angler is one of the greatest challenges in all of sport. Imagine for a moment how long it would take to become effective at say, basketball, or golf (or any other sport for that matter!) if you were blindfolded! What if you took shot after shot after shot and only got feedback when the ball went through the hoop, or in the hole? Without immediate visual feedback, it would take forever to develop proficiency. Consider this: there are a few musicians who can't see; there aren't any who can't hear!

Outcome Feedback

To begin with, think about two different types of feedback: outcome feedback and process feedback. Outcome feedback for anglers answers the question "Did this cast draw a strike?" Such feedback, as suggested, is very hard to get, as you often make dozens or hundreds of casts between bites. To complicate matters, when you do get bit, you can often only guess at which components of your presentation mattered, and which were irrelevant. Too bad you can't see fish turn away from a gold, double willowleaf chartreuse spinnerbait on one cast and then smash a silver, Colorado-bladed white one on the next! And while pros are fond of saying, "Let the fish tell you what they want," the message you and I most often hear from fish is, "Nope, I don't want that!" Especially with a tough bite, relying on outcome feedback from the fish is an exercise in futility.

However, if you have kept good records (remember the fishing log section in your **Psychology of Exceptional Fishing** notebook?!) over time, you can accumulate quite a bit of useful outcome feedback. Try this: Go back through your tournament notes and list the baits you used last year that gave you numbers of fish, and then look at the ones that gave you big fish. You might want to break this information down by season, pre-spawn, post-spawn, pre-summer, etc.

Also, look for patterns related to time of day, weather conditions, or lake levels. This exercise allows you to condense data, essentially eliminating unproductive casts and focusing only on those baits and presentations that resulted in strikes.

As suggested elsewhere, compare your tournament notes to the catch data of anglers whose skills and opinions you trust. However, even though there are a billion articles, books, and videotapes about what Larry, Kevin, and Guido use, in the end, you need feedback about what works for you.

Based on what you read in previous chapters, it's not news for me to say that getting accurate feedback from your notes hinges on being accurate and honest! Maybe you *occasionally* exaggerate the number or size of fish you caught when talking to your pals at work, but when it comes to building a fishing information database, don't fool yourself. If you only caught three short fish on a medium depth firetiger crankbait, so be it it. Reflecting on your feedback notes, you may decide this was the wrong presentation for a midsummer, clear-water tournament. You will draw the wrong conclusions, however, if what you write is unclear or inaccurate.

Process Feedback

Process feedback essentially involves paying attention to and working on the mechanics of *what* you are doing and *how* you are doing it. Top performers frequently talk about "getting back to basics", and you should consider this too. Focusing on process dimensions such as how you cast, flip, or pitch allows for one of the kinds of feedback you need to improve.

For example, how accurate is your casting, really? How about precision with flipping techniques? What about medium-range pitching? Maybe you should put a target in your backyard and make some casts, flips, and pitches from different distances and find out! Can you lay your jig on a tin pie plate five times out of six from twenty-five feet? How about on a coffee can cover? On a quarter!? Perceptual psychology tells us that accuracy is inversely related to the size of the target. That means that if you make your target small when practice casting, you will be more accurate when tournament time rolls around!

You've also heard this before, but maybe *now* is the time to test your lures in a swimming pool. Outside pools in southern states are too cold for swimming during the winter anyway, so take some favorite lures poolside and see what they do with different retrieves. Does your favorite crankbait really back up when you stop reeling, just like the ad says it should? If you live where pools are drained and lakes are frozen, talk with the custodian of the local community center or high school. Maybe you can trade a fishing trip for some after-hours pool time that only the two of you need to know about!

Bottom line, put your pride on the sidelines and ask a couple of fellow competitors for honest feedback. You might be surprised at what the top guy in your club thinks about your jig fishing or your approach to jerkbaits. Just don't rely exclusively on the fish to tell you how you're doing. Finding creative was to get feedback allows you to accurately evaluate your performance, a key step on the way to the top.

Revise

Just like you need to annually review your commitments, your practical skills, your internal resources, and your goals, revising your practice plans at regular intervals also makes sense. At a minimum, you should create a practice plan every six months. Think about it historically. If you had been honing a new technique every six months for the last three years, what would your skill set look like today? Looking ahead, if your goal is to be a top competitor, you don't want the *next* six months to slide by without making at least one important improvement, do you?

Change

Top athletes everywhere are admired for the speed and accuracy with which they change. I loved watching Michael Jordan when he had the basketball in his hands. Guys like Kobe Bryant, Allan Iverson, and Carmelo Anthony are also good, but MJ was the best! When he took off for the hoop, you just never knew *what* he was going to do, but you could be pretty sure it wasn't what he did last time! Like all great athletes, he could change and adapt *instantly* to whatever circumstances came his way.

You could and should bring a change-oriented attitude to your fishing, especially your practice sessions. Try taking a timer or a stopwatch with you in the boat, and when you're practicing, set it for five minutes. When the alarm goes off, change something. Alter your retrieve speed, change colors, try a new lure, or pick a different casting angle. And set the timer for five more minutes. Then change again. Keep in mind this famous saying: "There is nothing more foolish than doing the same thing over and over, and expecting different results." If you're not sure what to do, change something!

My daughter Dorothy was about seven when Steve and I took her on the river for a spring walleye trip. The customary lift-drop technique with a jig-and-minnow failed to produce a single bite, though we kept at it. Finally my daughter said,"I'm just gonna hold my minnow *real still*". How cute! It wasn't until after Dorothy had caught three fish that Steve and I realized we needed to change and hold our minnows *real still*, too!

REGULAR GUY TIP

So you're comfortable with the way you fish, and you don't want to make too many changes. Okay, fine. Just try this. The next time your boat partner outfishes you, see if you can't figure out *something* he is doing that you're not and try that. You can learn *one* more good fishing technique, can't you?

CHAPTER 12

Relaxation Exercises:
How To Be Calm *And* Alert!

The next several chapters describe specific performance techniques you can use to improve your mental approach to fishing. Top athletes, astute observers, and analysts in all sports talk about the importance of "relaxed concentration" as a foundational dimension for exceptional performance. Here's how the relaxation part works.

The best way to illustrate the importance of relaxation in a complex, demanding sport like competitive fishing is to consider what performance looks like when you are not relaxed. Here, you can either use your own experience or the television coverage of tournaments to know that people who are emotionally distraught, tense, or stressed-out do not always think clearly or act appropriately! Sometimes my lure lands in a bush because I just made a lousy cast, though like most of you, my best "tree bass" were hooked on days when I was really upset! Familiar sayings like "cool under pressure", "calm in the heat of competition" or "poised in the face of difficulty" illustrate the importance of maintaining your emotional equilibrium in order to think clearly and perform efficiently.

And while you may be able to tell me what kinds of people or circumstances calm you down or make you upset, you may not appreciate how much *internal control* you have over your feelings.

Deep Breathing

Focusing on and adjusting your breathing is an important element in most relaxation exercises. However, did you know that breathing exercises by themselves can be deeply relaxing?

Exercise 12: Basic Relaxation

Try this exercise: find a place where you can sit quietly for five minutes. If you can't do it right now without being interrupted, wait until later

63

today or this evening. Find a comfortable place to sit, put both feet flat on the floor, and let your hands and forearms rest comfortably in your lap.
Now close your eyes and breathe in through your nose. Just pay attention to the feeling of the air coming into your lungs through your nasal passages. Then exhale through your mouth. Don't try to do anything else at first; just pay attention to what your breathing feels like. Once again, breathe in through your nose and exhale through you mouth. Pay close attention to what the air feels like as it fills your lungs, and again as it goes out. See if you notice your chest expanding or your shoulders rising and falling as the air fills you up and empties out. Concentrate on six breaths in a row—quietly count to three as you breathe in through your nose; then count to four as you breathe through your mouth.(I know, the numbers don't add up...not to worry...you won't run out of air!) Breathe in through your nose; breathe out through your mouth. Do this six times.

What you will probably notice is by the sixth repetition, your breathing has become slightly deeper and slower. This happens to almost everyone.

Now take a breath and consciously breathe in a little deeper (count to four) and exhale a litter longer (use a 5 or 6 count). Try holding your breath for a moment after you have inhaled fully before you begin to exhale. Try that again. Breathe in a litter deeper than you would normally, hold it for a second or two, and then breathe out more fully than you normally would. Try that three or four times.

Now try breathing just slightly slower than you have before. Continue to take in the same amount of air, only instead of inhaling quickly; try to bring the air in through your nose slowly. Hold your breath for two seconds, and then exhale fully yet deliberately. Try that again. Breathe in through your nose slowly and deeply. Hold it for two seconds, and breathe out slowly and deliberately through your mouth.

As you do this, notice any changes in muscle tension throughout in your body. Many individuals describe noticing less tension in their hands, or in their shoulders. Some people note decreased tension in their facial muscles. There isn't anything that you "should" experience with this exercise. However, I encourage you to experiment with this breathing exercise and see what happens. You might feel a little funny doing this on your own, especially at first. However, you have probably seen many other top athletes use this technique, although in abbreviated form. At both college and professional levels, it is common to see basketball players at the free throw line, and pitchers as well as hitters in baseball, as well as Olympic track and field athletes take a series of deep breaths before they move into action. If this exercise works for them, it can work for you, don't you think?

Muscle Relaxation

In conjunction with deep breathing, many people find specific muscle relaxation exercises valuable. One common method involves tightening and then releasing specific muscles. There are several variations of this technique; here's how one of them works.

Exercise 13: Muscle Relaxation

Once again, find a quiet place to sit comfortably for five minutes. Begin breathing in through your nose and out through your mouth, as before, slowing and deliberately. However, this time, as you breathe in, clench your left fist as tight as you can. When you have finished inhaling, hold your breath for two seconds and tighten your fist even more.

Now, quickly release the tension in your hand, spread your fingers, and exhale slowly and completely. As you exhale in a slow, deliberate way let go of all the tension in your left hand. Repeat this process with your right hand. Breathe in slowly while clenching your right hand into a very tight fist. Hold your breath for two seconds and tighten your fist more, and then release the tension in your hand quickly while breathing out in a measured, deliberate, complete way. Do this three more times, and notice the tension in your hand change!

As with the rest of the specific performance techniques I will illustrate, you will get the most out of these relaxation exercises if you find a trained professional to help you get started. Experienced relaxation therapists or a sport psychologist will guide you through these and other relaxation exercises and demonstrate how to relax many different muscle groups. Interestingly, there are almost no negative side effects associated with doing relaxation exercises, beyond the fact that some people get so relaxed they fall asleep! While these exercises can help you be more relaxed right now, a substantial body of research speaks to the cumulative benefit of such techniques. In other words, the more you do these relaxation exercises, the more relaxed you are likely to be on a regular basis.

Here's an interesting insight. Baseball pitchers on the mound often have television cameras right in their faces, and you can see them take two or three deep breaths before they move into action. What you don't see is the rest of their routine that sets up the deep breaths. So try this: when you do deep breathing exercise at home, first envision yourself picking up your rod and reel. Then, just before you make a cast (like just before you would make the pitch!) take two deep breaths. Like I said, if it works for Roger Clemens and Johan Santana, it will probably work for you!

Crisis Management

Certainly you can use deep breathing exercises in direct response to a crisis. There are numerous stories about Olympic and professional athletes who responded to a poor performance by doing a series of relaxation exercises that allowed them to successfully compete in the next event. Competitive fishermen, in response to lost fish, equipment failures, or errors in judgment can also use relaxation exercises to regain their emotional equilibrium.

These are only two of the many relaxation techniques available. However, remember this: when you are relaxed, you will be able to think more clearly, make better decisions, and cast more accurately than when you are tense or frustrated.

REGULAR GUY TIP

So you probably think deep breathing exercises are flaky, or stupid, or worse! Well, you'd be wrong there. Turn on your TV and find an NBA game. Watch what those guys do before they shoot free throws. They each have a mental routine that involves looking at the same spot on the rim, bouncing the ball the same number of times, and taking the same number of *deep breaths* before each shot. Why? Because deep breathing works. (If you're still sure you're right, tell Carmelo Anthony deep breathing is flaky or stupid!)

CHAPTER 13

Concentration Methods:
How Paying Attention Pays Off!

Question #1: Have you ever missed a strike, or lost a good fish because you were paying attention to something other than fishing?

Question #2: Have you ever messed up in a tournament and lost money because of a clear lapse in concentration?

If you said no to both questions, you can stop reading. This chapter is for the rest of us!

Attention and Concentration

Before proceeding, let me begin by stating some obvious yet important ideas. First, artfully presenting a bait or lure in a way that causes a fish to strike is a difficult and complex task. In some situations it's best to scan the environment quickly, rapidly assemble information, shift your focus, and immediately adjust to changing dimensions such as weather, current, and baitfish movement. However, especially during the bait-delivery/casting process, focused attention and concentration are absolutely essential for success. Do you present your lures blind-folded, or with your eyes closed? Do you flip, pitch, or cast while watching water skiers or gazing at sun bathers? Well, of course not. No one is foolish enough to do *that*!

However, while you are probably good at concentrating on where and how you cast your lure, attention can *easily* wander during the retrieve. Once that bait disappears beneath the surface and visual contact is lost, you are at risk to become distracted by unimportant sights, sounds, or activities.

When using topwater baits, casting to visible cover, or when sight fishing you almost never take your eyes off your lure. You focus very closely on exactly what your bait is doing throughout the retrieve. Imagine how much more efficient and effective you would be if you used that same intense attention and concentration with jigs, spinnerbaits, and crankbaits.

Here are three concentration exercises, each involving 5 casts, to experiment with and practice. See which one of these works best for you. Begin by getting your boat wet. Before each exercise, tell yourself you will give your undivided attention to the *next cast and retrieve*. Don't expect yourself to pay attention to every cast for the rest of the afternoon. Remember, during these exercises or during fishing you really only have to concentrate closely on one cast: the *next cast*!

Exercise 14: Imagery Awareness

Pick a small target and send your bait to it. This can be a bush, a rock, a current break, or a weedline. Now, to paraphrase a silly saying, "Be the Bait." Imagine you are your lure as it hops, crawls, and/or swims back to the boat. Pay attention to what your lure feels like as you vary your retrieve speed; monitor the tension and the resistance on your line; feel the weight and vibration of your bait as it comes back to you. Then, make another cast and do the same thing; pay very close attention to exactly what your bait feels like throughout the retrieve. Make three more casts using the same focused concentration.

This retrieve exercise will only take a few minutes. However, you may end up gaining valuable information about what it feels like to "be the bait". One thing you *will* notice is that you can't *be the bait* and pay attention to water skiers at the same time!

Exercise 15: Tactile Awareness

Make another careful cast (remember, the smaller your target, the better your casting accuracy), and this time pay specific attention to the structure or cover you are fishing. See, feel, and imagine the ledge, the lay down branches, or the grass as your bait comes over and through it. Slow down, and let your lure give you as much information as it can about the depth, the bottom composition, and the thickness or composition of the cover you're fishing. Let yourself be curious about what your bait is running into beneath the surface. Do this exercise five times as well; see if you don't pick up more information on the fifth cast than you did on the first!

Exercise 16: Sightless Awareness

After another precise cast, close your eyes as you retrieve your bait. See what you notice on *this* retrieve. Visually handicapped people develop heightened sensory awareness allowing them to feel, hear, and smell better than the rest of us. They can sense in other ways what they cannot see. With practice, you can do the same. Remember the last time you set the hook into a fish you really didn't know was there? This exercise will help you catch more of *those* fish!

Take these techniques to the lake and give them a try, 5 casts each. Focused concentration is likely to improve if you do.

Away from the Lake

You can also practice attention and concentration exercises at home or at work. Pick out a common item like a dish rag or a magazine cover and examine it very closely. You might use a kitchen timer for this exercise, giving yourself, say, three minutes to notice as many details as you can about what you are looking at. Some people like to make a list of everything they notice.

I heard a fascinating story a couple of months ago from a pro angler that illustrated this practice-attention-and-concentration-at-home technique. She was finishing a shopping trip when the elevator she was in got stuck between the second and first floors. It was the middle of the day, the elevator people called right away on the emergency phone, and as a result, she wasn't really panicked, just annoyed at being delayed. "So, I'm standing there with my shopping bag in one hand and my keys in the other, and with nothing else to do, I began looking closely at my keys.

"As I did, I remembered your suggestion about practicing concentration at home, and I began noticing some subtle yet important differences in the keys I have carried around with me for several years. My house key and my office key are the same color and type, made by the same company. I am constantly choosing the wrong one, especially when I'm in a hurry! As I stood there in the elevator looking, (and finally seeing!) I noticed that my office key is about a 16th of an inch *longer* than my house key! It wasn't a big enough difference to be obvious until by paying close attention I saw it. Now, it's a very clear difference and it's easy for me to pick the right key!"

These exercises do several things for you: they help focus your attention, they help tune out distractions, and they encourage looking beyond the obvious. In other words, they sharpen your powers of observation. I can hear some of you saying, "Doing one exercise won't help me concentrate better." OK, fine; this one exercise, done one time, won't. However, try thinking of it like lifting weights. One weightlifting session won't make you stronger. However, three sessions a week for six weeks will!

REGULAR GUY TIP

Even if you don't want to spend a bunch of time practicing attention and concentration exercises, try this: the next time you're fishing deep with a Texas-rigged plastic worm, or a Lindy rig, or a spoon, pretend you're fishing on the surface. Just for a minute, see if you can picture what your bait looks like down there on the bottom of the lake. Doing this, even for 60 seconds, forces you to pay closer attention to your fishing. And these are the seconds that could make all the difference!

CHAPTER 14

Visualization:
Get The Picture?

Arguably the most consistent competitor under pressure, Jack Nicklaus was also one of the pioneers in using visualization to improve athletic performance. In his talks and in his writing, Nicklaus explained how he would envision each shot in his mind before he took it. He would see in his mind his swing, as well as the flight of his ball, and he often attributed his remarkable success in pressure-packed tournaments to this visualization technique. Hundreds of performance psychology studies support what Jack believed and taught.

Interestingly, of our five senses, vision is the one over which we have the most voluntary control. If we taste, feel, smell, or hear something we don't like, it is very difficult to effectively block out that sensory experience. Yet if we see something unpleasant, we can instantly close our eyes and mentally shut it out; hence the phrase "Out of sight, out of mind." Happily, the converse of this is also true; that is, it's not *too difficult* to create a clear, detailed visual picture of a thing or person or event that is not near at hand.

Even more fascinating is the human capacity to create a visual image of something you have never experienced before. It might not be particularly accurate, but you *could* visualize a picture of yourself walking on the Moon, for example. In this chapter, you will discover how to harness the power of visual images to become a better angler.

Outcome Visualization

Mention visualization to the average fishing fanatic, and you will likely hear about the picture he or she has in mind of catching a 10 lb. walleye, or a 30 lb. catfish, or a 22 lb-*5 oz.* largemouth bass! If you're talking to competitive anglers, the visual image will be of him or her on stage holding a large trophy or a big check! To be sure, it is worthwhile to envision winning or placing high in each tournament. Sometimes visualization may even influence an outcome. I'm not sure how often this happens, but the following *is* a true story!

In the predawn stillness of a tournament finale, I overheard a co-angler tell his pro partner he envisioned them catching twenty-two pounds that day. I saw the pro smile, though I couldn't hear if he said anything in response. However, eight hours later at the weigh-in, I watched in amazement as the display flashed 21.96 lbs for their fish! Coincidence? Premonition? Self-fulfilling prophecy? Who knows? I do know the angler who envisioned that outcome, and he'd sure like to be able to do that more often!

Anecdotes aside, most of the research on visualization as an effective psychological tool focuses on creating and practicing mental pictures that can help us improve attitudes and techniques, not outcomes.

Technique Visualization

Numerous performance psychology research articles point out the value of visualizing specific behaviors as a way to improve them. College students, for example, who use visualization to practice shooting free throws on a basketball court show improved accuracy that is nearly equal to the improvement obtained by those who spend the same amount of time physically shooting free throws. Track athletes can train themselves to envision exactly how they will run a specific race. In exquisite detail, they go through each segment of their race, from coming out of the blocks to crossing the finish line. Similar data support improvement for athletes using visualization techniques in sports such as baseball, tennis, and figure skating, to name just a few.

You can also use visualization to improve your effectiveness. Consider this: Think of a specific technique you have been trying to improve with physical practice. One top competitor I worked with had difficulty learning to fish soft plastic stick baits because he was too impatient with them. He couldn't/wouldn't let this lure sink for more than about two seconds before he moved it. We talked through some different options. He finally settled on a visualization technique where he saw himself cast the lure out, and then envisioned himself standing patiently for ten seconds while the bait slowly descended through the water column. Using this in combination with the deep breathing and relaxation exercises discussed in **Chapter 12**, he was eventually able to train himself to effectively fish stick baits slowly, and in progressively deeper water. You could probably do something similar yourself.

Let's say you have been trying to improve your flippin' accuracy. As stated in earlier chapters, before using any mental exercise, make sure you have adequate, balanced equipment. You need a rod heavy enough, long enough, and comfortable enough to get the job done, a quality reel that can be adjusted with precision, and a lure and line that work well together. (Never, ever think that mental exercises will overcome lousy equipment or poor preparation! They will not!) Once you have a good set of tools in hand, practice flippin' to a nearby target. Within a few minutes, you are likely to make a perfect or a near perfect flip. Congratulations! Now you are ready to put visualization in play.

Exercise 17: Visual Practice

Instead of trying to physically duplicate that last flip, set your rod down, and spend a few minutes with your eyes closed visually repeating what you just did. Watch yourself pull your line back, notice your arms swing out, and see your bait move forward to the target. Observe the position of your rod, your reel, and your thumb on the reel spool.

If you have a vivid visual sense, this technique may be easy to do. Most anglers, whether they fish tournaments or not, have pretty good skills for creating and using visual images. However, it is unlikely that your visualization skills are fully developed. In a variety of settings, such as when it comes to putting a lure in a tight spot, controlling an acrobatic fish, or driving your boat through rough water, visualization practices can help you learn and remember what you look like at your best.

To be sure, I am *not* suggesting that you *only* rely on visualization techniques. However, I frequently hear, from both professional and amateur anglers, something like this: "You know Doc, it's really fun to play these visual pictures over in my head when at home, on the road, or in my motel room. I can't tell you *how*, but I just *know* they're helping me!" Even if visualization exercises only increase your *confidence* in a particular skill area, that makes them worth trying, right?

Use the following table to list four or five techniques. Then create and practice a clear visual image for each. In the first column write down the technique you would like to improve. In the second column, make notes about what perfect execution of this technique looks like. Try to think of a time or place when you performed this technique flawlessly. In the third column, note how often you visually practice this technique.

73

Exercise 18: VISUALIZATION

Technique	Visual Image	Practice Dates

Visually Reprogram Mistakes

Visualization can also used to reprogram mistakes. Anglers tell me this particular type of visualization is both fun and helpful. My favorite example of this technique is a personal one, so I will tell you about that.

I hooked my first national tournament bass on Lake Wheeler from the rear deck of O.T. Fears's boat. Looking back, it was clear I was wound tighter than a two-dollar watch when that 3 lb. largemouth slammed my crankbait about four feet from the boat. Like the nervous rookie I was, I froze and hung on tight, while the fish jumped twice and pulled off. Initially, I replayed that mistake over and over in my mind until a sport psychologist friend of mine told me to create a visual image of that scene in which I did the *right* thing. I tried this, and found it was much more fun to envision myself calmly hitting the free spool button, giving the fish some line, and yelling for the net!

Exercise 19: Visualize The Correct Way

Try this yourself! Pick a mistake from last year, and replay it in your mind. Instead of making the mistake again, envision what you should/could/would do differently. Once you have a visual picture of the correct way to handle the situation, review it again and again until it becomes part of your consciousness. About two years after my Lake Wheeler experience, I was fishing a fall riprap pattern when a nice fish ate my jig right at the boat. Without thinking, the image I had created of this scene kicked in, and I pushed the free spool and let him run. Then, I turned to my brother Brian and said, "O. T., get the net!" I'm sure he thought I was goofy, but I knew then.....this visualization stuff works!

Another talented, yet high-strung competitive angler I worked with told me he was at his worst on tournament mornings just before take off. At such times he felt tense, apprehensive, and fretful. Even on those days when he was doing well in the tournament, or when he had good fish located, he still found himself ill-at-ease waiting to start the day. "Once I run to my first spot and make a few casts, I seem to settle down, though that pre-takeoff hour is miserable," he told me.

We began by practicing the relaxation exercises from **Chapter 12**. After he was able to put himself in a relaxed state, I asked him to visualize different parts of his routine prior to take off. In a relaxed state, he envisioned waking up in his camper and getting dressed. Then he went through the process of getting his boat in the water and motoring to the takeoff point. It was at this point his relaxed feelings went away, and his anticipatory worry and apprehension seemed to take over.

I helped him regain his relaxed mood, and asked him to visualize easing himself into the tournament staging area. Using what we call in psychology a successive approximation process, he was eventually able to envision sitting in his boat without too much tension.

As we talked about this scenario, the root cause of his worry surfaced. "I get it! I know what I'm doing," he suddenly realized, "I'm looking at all the other competitors and assuming they are on better fish than I am!" It became quite obvious that if he remained focused on himself, his own boat and tackle, and his co-angler he stayed pretty relaxed. However, if he began looking around, his anticipatory anxiety started to build. By creating and practicing a positive, relaxed visual image he was able to transform his mental state in this situation!

Visualize a Positive Mental State

One of the most popular uses of visualization is to create positive mental images of what being successful looks and feels like.

One top professional I worked with described himself as calm, relaxed, and open-minded during practice, and uptight, tense, and constricted in his thinking once the tournament started. He had some difficulty understanding how he was different on practice days versus tournament days, so I asked him to sit down with his two children and draw a picture of what he looked like on his best day. He told me he thought this was a silly exercise, but he was willing to do it as a project with his kids.

Then I asked him to draw a similar picture of what he looked like on his worst day. However, before he even finished this assignment, he called to tell me what a dramatic experience it was. "Drawing this picture clearly made me feel frustrated, aggravated, and upset," he said. "My wife even came over a couple of times and asked me what was wrong!" In doing this visualization exercise (with the help of construction paper and his children's magic markers!) this pro discovered that instead of fishing with an open, relaxed mind, his mental state on tournament day was almost entirely on the embarrassment he expected to feel when he weighed in with an empty bag. In his case, the only good tournament day was one that started out with nice fish right off the bat. Even a small amount of fishless time drew him into a negative, worrisome, anxious, emotional state that eroded his confidence and effectiveness.

Fortunately, it was relatively easy for him to take the positive mental image he had of himself in practice and apply it to what he wanted to be like on tournament days. Here again, repeatedly practicing a positive visual image helped make this emotional transfer happen smoothly and permanently. Visual images can do the same for you!

REGULAR GUY TIP

Tell one of your fishing pals the story about your best trip. Fill in all the details. There, you just created a visual image for him! If you create those same detailed images for yourself, it will help you catch more fish!

CHAPTER 15

Mental Rehearsal:
Practice In Your Head First!

Mental Rehearsal, quite simply, works. In the previous chapter on visualization, you learned how creating, using, and practicing positive mental images can improve your fishing. These mental pictures are designed to make you feel better as well as help you fish better. Mental rehearsal is a similar process, though the focus here is on repeatedly using mental pictures, words, and internal checklists to increase efficiency and effectiveness. As with other performance psychology exercises, there are many types of mental rehearsal techniques that a good sport psychologist can help you explore. Here are two that are universally effective.

Mental Checklists

The first time I observed the mental checklist technique was in high school, about a zillion years ago. I was talking with my math teacher after school one day, and when we got up to leave, he paused at the door with a kind of blank look on his face. After a few seconds he turned around, went back, opened his desk drawer, and picked up his car keys. I asked him what happened that made him stop at the door and remember his keys. He told me he had gotten into the habit of pausing in that particular spot as he left for the day to go through his mental checklist. What he told me was this, "I go through a list in my head: keys, glasses, briefcase, watch, and coat. If I have those things, I know I'm good to go."

You can use the same process to improve your fishing success. Many anglers use mental checklists during the course of a fishing day. During practice for a national pro-am tournament, I watched a former world champion use a mental checklist sequence every time we changed spots. As we settled into our seats he would say to himself, sometimes barely audibly to me, "Rods strapped, kill switch attached, trolling motor secure, outboard trimmed, GPS map on." When I asked him if this mental checklist was still useful after all these years, he told me that just the week before he had avoided a collision with an underwater rockpile by remembering to switch to his GPS map. "I was on an unfamiliar lake, and my sonar said 14 foot," he explained. "But that was at the transom. Two boat lengths in front of me large boulders were covered by only 18 inches of water. On a calm, clear day, I might have seen those rocks before I climbed down off the bow, but that day was cloudy and windy. I would have needed a new prop and maybe a new lower unit if I hadn't gone through my mental checklist and flipped over to the GPS map before I put the hammer down."

Exercise 20: Mental Checklist

Create a mental checklist to use in situations you frequently encounter, like in the examples described above. Whether it involves launching or loading your boat, preparing for your next fishing trip, or using a particular psychological technique, make a mental list of steps to go through in order to be most effective. While I am certainly a fan of written records and checklists, as you can tell, it also helps to use mental checklists, at least for circumstances that are not too complicated.

Mental Preparation Images

If you have a reasonably clear game plan of how to approach an upcoming fishing trip or tournament, it can be quite helpful to create mental pictures of exactly when, where, how, and what you will be doing. If, for example, you are going to fish Sam Rayburn in February, traveling to East Texas will likely include mental practice casting with red rattle baits. Top professionals will also mentally practice switching to backup baits if "Texas Red" turns out to be the wrong color!

You could also rehearse in your mind varying the speed and angle of your retrieve every five casts. Feel free to mentally rehearse catching seven or eight pound bass, though I would recommend spending *most* of the time mentally rehearsing specific skills!

Mental rehearsal can also prepare you in other ways. You may already visualize and mentally review the travel route to your next tournament. Add to that by developing a mental picture of the parts of the lake you will fish on each practice day. Make this mental rehearsal picture come alive by traveling in your mind to the various stops on your practice route. Later, transfer these visually rehearsed images to a notebook, to your map, or to a pre-tournament practice list.

To be even more creative, go back to your list of goals in **Chapter 7** and develop mental pictures of what accomplishing each of your goals looks like. Research data says that having a mental picture of where you want to end up, and another mental picture of how you plan to get there significantly increases the likelihood that you will attain your goals. (You can't *begin to imagine* the number of times I mentally reviewed, edited, and rewrote each chapter of this book!!)

Mental rehearsal isn't all that complicated, as you can see by the examples I have used. If I knew more about you and your unique fishing style, I would be able to make detailed suggestions about specific mental rehearsal techniques that might work. What I will say is that professional and amateur athletes alike frequently use mental rehearsal techniques to improve performance. A brief consultation with a sport psychologist could result in a successful mental rehearsal schedule for you.

Affirmations

Performance psychology research studies show that positive self-statements, or self-talk, can help people feel relaxed, confident, and self-assured, mental conditions consistently associated with peak performance. However, the value of positive thinking and positive self-talk is often misrepresented. To be genuinely effective, research tells us, self-statements or affirmations need to be uplifting and also reasonable. Exaggerated statements like "I am the greatest" or "I'll win every tournament" rarely work. In fact, they are often counterproductive, setting you up for disappointment when your proclamations don't produce the intended results. When you don't win as you claimed, you look foolish, you may lose confidence in yourself, and you may abandon as useless positive affirmations, and also other helpful psychological techniques.

Instead, experiment with self-statements like, "I am fully prepared" or "In mind and body and spirit, I am ready for this tournament." or "I have what it takes to win." Play around with the words, as well as with your tone of voice until you find phrases or sentences that ring true. Repeat them to yourself several times. Try saying them out loud. Notice how they make you feel now. Affirmations can help create a positive mental framework that opens the door to clear thinking, to confident execution, and ultimately to peak performance!

Perhaps more importantly, positive self-statements are incompatible with worrisome, distracting, self-critical thoughts that can disrupt concentration and ultimately diminish effectiveness. Repeating affirmations slowly and thoughtfully for a couple of minutes, either before or during a fishing day can boost calmness *and* confidence.

And don't be intimidated by those flamboyant, public displays of boasting that masquerade as confidence. People who loudly and frequently assert their superior skills and accomplishments may sound invincible. However, such melodrama has little relationship to genuine confidence or sustained success. As you know from your own experience, talk by itself doesn't mean much!

REGULAR GUY TIP

To the "regular guy", mental images are pretty much the same as the memory pictures running around in your head. Here's an easy way to use them to improve your fishing. The next time you run into lousy fishing conditions, such is a cold front, or a seriously windy day, think back to a time when you got a few fish under similar circumstances. Then try to create or remember the picture of that day in your mind. If you do, you may end up with a much more positive attitude toward the difficult conditions facing you today!

CHAPTER 16

Stress Management Skills: Weathering Emotional Storms!

Everybody talks about stress and the importance of managing it, in fishing and in life. "That really stressed me out", "The conditions put a lot of stress on the fish", "Managing stress effectively is what separates good anglers from great anglers". Such comments are frequently heard. At the same time, there are many different opinions about exactly what "stress" is. One main difficulty is that what is dark and stressful to one person might be sunshine and happiness to another! Thirty mile an hour wind, for example, could be *very* stressful if you have a long run into it to get to your best fishing spot; that same wind could cause pure joy if you know that is where your competition is going, and you have a secluded cove near the launch site to fish!

Psychologists often use a physiological definition of stress as something that *disturbs or interferes with* the normal equilibrium of an individual. If you are prone to getting seriously stressed out in ways that interfere with your life, you would do well to seek professional assistance. Figuring out exactly what causes you stress, and finding an individualized treatment program would be the clear recommendations for anyone who has recurrent episodes of serious stress. For example, if you get painful/recurrent headaches, stomach aches, or muscle pain in response to stress, or if you experience significant amounts of tension, worry, depression, irritability, or frustration on a regular basis, you owe it to yourself to visit a mental health professional.

Okay, I had to say that because I'm a psychologist! Now let's talk about the usual day-to-day stresses of fishing!

Adaptively managing the stress of competition is crucial for any serious athlete. And clearly, competition is stressful. Maintaining poise under pressure is universally admired. When someone performs perfectly in a pressure-packed setting, we shake our heads, smile enviously, and ask: "How *does* she do it?" Well, *one* of the ways she does it is by remaining calm, relaxed, and stress-free so that she is able to use all of her best skills *at that moment*. Certainly there are individual differences in how people naturally process and deal with stress and pressure. However, there is no need to be limited to the coping skills you inherited. In fact, stress management techniques are among the easiest psychological skills to learn. This chapter will discuss stress management tactics from a practical standpoint, highlighting techniques applicable to both tournament and non-tournament anglers.

For this discussion, let's talk about three different kinds of athletic stress: anticipatory anxiety, performance pressure, and post-performance frustration. But first, let's deal with an important preliminary question.

How Much Stress is Too Much?

Popular wisdom tells us that a certain amount of stress is a good thing. There is much talk about how athletes need to get "psyched up" for The Big Game. However, this is more myth than reality when it comes to complex tasks like fishing. Performance psychology research tells us that stress, pressure, or pre-performance anxiety can easily interfere with successfully carrying out intricate, complicated mental and physical assignments. Even a small amount of stress can diminish a person's capacity to think clearly and logically, to accurately analyze information, and to make sound decisions.

Additionally, even minor mental turmoil can disrupt your ability to perform the intricate physical tasks that fishing requires. When you feel relaxed, you are able to be emotionally, behaviorally, and intellectually flexible. When you get stressed out, you can stubbornly zero in on one particular way of thinking, feeling, or behaving. You may also frantically and perhaps impulsively jump from one thing to the next, or make careless decisions based on anxiety and panic. I hear zillions of stories every year about anglers running up the wrong cove because they were preoccupied about getting to a hot spot before someone else, or trying to drive *over instead of around* an underwater gravel bed or sandbar for the same reason! And of course I don't suppose *you* ever did anything stupid to your boat or motor because you were upset about a squabble at home!

Awhile back my neighbor got into an Animated Domestic Conversation (ADC) with his significant other, said something to the effect of "gol darn, honey, I think I'll go fishin'", and then too hurriedly tied the boat to the truck and drove off....forgetting to elevate and brace his motor. Now he has a really cute skeg scratch down the middle of his driveway to go with the $242 repair bill. It's that line in the driveway, however, that will remind him of his ADC, *and* of how difficult it is to think of all that is important when you're stressed out!

So you want to be stress-free while you're *catching* fish, but more importantly you need freedom from inner turmoil to think clearly enough to *find* the fish. You don't need me to tell you that figuring out where the fish are and what they want to bite *today* is infinitely more difficult than landing them. Since you aspire to be a premier angler, the more relaxed and stress-free you become, the better you will function on the water.

Recognizing the Stress of Competition

Most fishing involves competition. You might use the sociological definition of competition as a rivalry between two or more persons for a desired object, or the psychological definition of a struggle between organisms (you and the fish!). Either way, fishing is competitive!

I used to jog with a group that included well-known watercolor artist, George M. Pope. We were running along the shore of Lake Superior on a warm spring morning when one guy commented he thought he ran faster when he was with the rest of us than he did when he ran by himself. Even though we were just running for "exercise", he felt it was like a race. There was a pause, and Geo said, "Don't kid yourself; if there is more than one person running, it's a race." And so it is with fishing.

You might *think* you don't fish competitively just because you don't do tournaments. Perhaps you say you're just out there for fun, that all you really want to do is enjoy being on the water in the boat with your buddies, watching the water skiers, blah, blah, blah! Well, I *seriously* doubt you can hold on to that attitude if the guy in the back of the boat is catching one fish after another and you are not! Even at a friendly level there is almost always a certain amount of competition between anglers. And there is *most assuredly* a serious competition going on between you and the fish! Think about it this way. If every time you went fishing the fish won, you would eventually take up golf!

Anticipatory Anxiety

For many, just preparing for a fishing trip, or for a competitive fishing event can be stressful. Even with primo preparation, you can become stressed out thinking about whether the fish will be where they're supposed to be, whether or not the weather will hold, whether the color or style of bait that worked last week will still work today, and so forth. I am sure you have your own list of things to worry about before a fishing trip; it's endless, really. If you have this type of anticipatory stress or anxiety, you need tactics to become emotionally calm and focused in order to perform at your best.

Performance Pressure

Once the fishing day begins, it's not difficult to become stressed out by circumstances that unfold. If the fish don't bite for the first four hours of an eight-hour trip, for example, most people will feel stressed. Losing a big fish is stressful for almost everyone as well. Whether or not there is money on the line, a hawg is a hawg, right? And if you lose a big fish because of a bad knot, or because the drag on the reel was set too tight, or because of a fundamental flaw in your character ☺, you may begin to feel *really* stressed-out!

Disappointment, frustration, and aggravation are common emotional reactions in this situation. You are also likely to become stressed or distraught if external circumstances conspire to separate you from that Very Large Fish. An especially mean-spirited VLF may choose to tangle your line in a sunken tree or wrap it around your trolling motor prop! Alternately, the guy you *thought* was a good fishing buddy may "accidentally" knock your VLF off the hook with the net!

In such situations, managing stress may be as simple as identifying and solving a problem that caused the stress in the first place. The realization that your VLF is no longer with you may yet be painful, though if you identify a practical reason why this occurred and fix it, you may feel better. A couple of summers ago, in the waning minutes of a tournament, *one of us* lost a nice fish because he forgot to trim the skirt on his jig. Instead of throwing a temper tantrum or smashing the light pole on his boat, he put the scissors to work, fixed the problem, and pitched to a few more bushes in time to get the fish that filled our limit.

Post-Performance Frustration

Once the fishing day is done, whether a tournament day or not, you may be the type of person who spends a fair amount of time rehashing what happened. In a general sense this is a good technique, since reviewing each day can help consolidate what you learned and perhaps generate ideas for what you could do better next time. However, after a bad day you may also have the tendency to remain in a frustrated, aggravated state, upset with yourself, the weatherman, or that obnoxious jet skier who kept buzzing your boat! A prolonged stress reaction may interfere with your ability to calmly return home or comfortably interact with other people in your life. One tournament angler's wife lamented, "You know, if Joe (not his real name) has a bad tournament, he is difficult to live with for about three days afterwards." Such a prolonged post-fishing stress reaction is not only unnecessary, it's probably not good for you.

For some, as suggested, the stress of fishing may cause racing heart rate, muscle tension, and headaches or stomach distress. A long, difficult day on the water can lead to emotional as well as physical fatigue. One top tournament angler I worked with would get so stressed out that he frequently caught a cold before or just after fishing trips. It wasn't until the coughing, sneezing, and nose-blowing caused him to miss some fish that he began to appreciate how the physical consequences of stress were hurting him. Clearly an important first step in managing the stress associated with fishing involves recognizing what outward manifestations of stress look like in your case and noticing the circumstances in which they are likely to occur.

Put another way, we all have "hot buttons". You know, the things, the people, and the circumstances that fairly predictably cause tension, apprehension, and irritability. Spend some time thinking about what your "hot buttons" are, and write them down in your **Psychology of Exceptional Fishing** notebook. Additionally, ask a couple of your fishing buddies what they think stresses you out. As in other domains, self-awareness and self-monitoring, while good starting points, do not always provide a complete or accurate picture. Nevertheless, if you recognize your "hot buttons" and see them coming, you can put steps in place to avoid them or limit their impact.

Stress Management Techniques

There are many kinds of stress management tactics available, and there are dozens of books in the self-help section of the library and bookstore that can give you ideas and advice. As mentioned, a sport psychologist can be especially helpful in tailoring these techniques to make them specifically applicable to your situation. Here are two that work for most everyone.

Let's say you have identified pre-fishing trip worry as a primary source of stress. On your way to the lake you typically feel nervous, tense, and apprehensive, and for no good reason. Your preparation has been thorough, a solid game plan is in place, and you have checked and rechecked your equipment. Fundamentally you have done all you can reasonably do to prepare. The problem is, you feel about as tense as if you were going after a Great White Shark with a Zebco 202!

Exercise 21: Managing Pre-Trip Stress

On your next fishing trip, try this: Begin by adopting a problem-solving attitude. Do you have and use a fishing trip checklist; or, have you tried to keep all of the different pre-trip variables in your head? If you don't have a checklist, I'm almost inclined to say you deserve whatever pre-trip worry you experience, but since I'm a nice guy, I won't say that. What I will say is, if you don't have a fishing trip checklist, then *make one now!*

Okay, so let's say you have a checklist made, and let's say you typically rely on it. But you're still worried. Take some time to think about, talk out, and write down your worries. It may help to refer back to **Chapter 8**, the section on controllable and uncontrollable variables. Are you principally concerned about variables you can control, but have not addressed, or, are you mostly apprehensive about variables over which you have little control?

If you're mostly concerned about controllable variables, then maybe the thing to do is rewrite your fishing trip checklist to include tactics that will handle these controllable variables. If worry and tension center on uncontrollable variables, then I would suggest a different approach. Instead of trying to solve a problem you can't control, try this option.

Once you notice your pre-trip anxiety starting up, sit in your boat, (or let your buddy drive), for the first five minutes. During this time, try the relaxation exercise from **Chapter 12**. Start by taking a long, deep breath. Count to three as you breathe in through your nose, and then count to four as you breathe out through your mouth. Then do it five more times. It takes about ten seconds to take this type of deep breath, so you can do six breaths in a minute. Thirty deep breaths will take a total of five minutes. You might find yourself distracted by random thoughts while doing this exercise. Don't worry about it; just go back to paying specific attention to how you're breathing.

As we discussed earlier, this exercise works especially well if you can sit in a comfortable chair, in quiet spot, and so forth. Some people like to do this exercise with their eyes closed. However, it also works just as well with your eyes open driving down the highway or sitting in your boat. Remember, deep breathing is not exactly obvious, so you don't have to worry about your buddy or anyone else watching and thinking you are some New Age Wacko; but even if someone does think that, so what? You probably fish with pink and white walleye jigs or cotton candy colored floating bass worms, right? Well, those lures are a lot goofier than deep breathing, and not nearly as effective at decreasing stress!

Exercise 22: Managing Frustration

As sure as the sun comes up in the East, the day will come when your fishing just flat stinks! Everything that can possibly go wrong does, and you end up skunked, zeroed, or as Sarah would say, DFL (Dead Freaking Last!) Now what? Thinking happy thoughts or humming a cheery tune doesn't really cut it when your stringer is empty and your buddies have out-fished you all day! Post fishing trip aggravation happens to all of us; rest assured that the guy who says he's never been shut out either doesn't fish, or doesn't tell the truth!

Fundamentally, you really can't stop those stressed or distraught feelings after a lousy day on the water. So don't try. Instead, go ahead and be bummed out, and if you can find someone willing to listen, whine, grouse, and complain—but only for a while. Instead of letting it go on and on, structure these stressful, disappointed, frustrated feelings by setting a certain time frame to be upset, say an hour or so. Then turn the page, so to speak, and move on.

Essentially you would do the same thing after a great day. A swell fishing trip typically ends with some excited conversation in the boat ramp parking lot, a few pictures, and congratulations all around. Perhaps there is a gathering at a local watering hole, and some bragging to other anglers. Then, after about an hour or two, you and your buddies start talking about the *next* trip. Use this same Timeframe Technique when faced with the stress of an embarrassing outing. You might be surprised at the result.

For both exercises, use your **Psychology of Exceptional Fishing** notebook to record what happens. The deep breathing exercise described earlier can be immediately as well as cumulatively beneficial. Using relaxation exercises for five or ten minutes three times a week can have significant positive effects on your overall well-being, as well as on your fishing effectiveness. Additionally, make notes about the Timeframe Technique and the circumstances in which you tried it. You'll end up with a record of how and when this technique worked and when it didn't. Remember, relaxed concentration is the goal. Identify your "hot buttons", breathe deeply, and let stress drift downstream.

REGULAR GUY TIP

Stress management exercises are for sissies, you say. Think what you want. However, consider this: no matter who you are, you don't fish as well when you're angry or upset as you do when you're not. So think about the most upsetting person or situation you encountered last year and try to avoid that person or that situation this year. You will save yourself some grief and aggravation, and you may catch an extra fish or two.

CHAPTER **17**

Optimal Intensity:
Too Much Passion or Not Enough?

Most of the Performance Psychology topics presented thus far rest on years, sometimes decades, of supporting research data. However, when it comes to Optimal Intensity, investigators typically rely on stories or incidental reports from individuals in different kinds of competition. And for good reason; it's no longer considered ethical to manipulate an individual's emotional intensity in order to do research! However, even though formal studies are few, there are recurring themes that illustrate how Optimal Intensity can positively influence fishing success.

In The Zone

The common term for Optimal Intensity is being "In The Zone", that unique, fleeting psychological state where peak performance occurs. Across many sports, competitors who have been in this state report remarkably similar experiences. Almost without exception, people describe a feeling of time slowing down. Some say they feel as though they are moving in slow motion, even when their actual speed is not diminished in the slightest. Commonly, performers describe a feeling of invincibility, the notion that no matter what happens, things will turn out for the best.

Athletes "In The Zone" say this level of optimal intensity includes an unusual or even eerie combination of quiet concentration and electric intensity that's difficult to describe. When competing in this state, individuals report being oblivious to distractions, such as crowd noise, or the behavior of fellow competitors. Many feel as if they are in a world of their own. In this frame of mind, they become completely focused on the task at hand. Additionally, most performers describe being essentially indifferent to the outcome of their performance. Yet at the same time, and not surprisingly, competitors are often at their very best while "In The Zone". It is both mysterious and frustrating that this optimal level of intensity frequently seems to arise out of nowhere, exist for an indefinite, though usually short period of time, and then disappear as quickly and completely as it arrived.

A few individuals believe they can create this unique internal experience at will, though sport psychologists are skeptical of such claims. There are some common ideas about what predisposes people to being "In The Zone", however. Greater agreement exists about what optimal emotional intensity is not. Let's look at this latter domain first.

Extreme Emotionality

Pre-competition routines for many professional as well as amateur athletes, as television graphically illustrates, frequently involve "pumping up" rituals. In many athletic events it's not unusual to find a good deal of whooping, hollering, and carrying on before and during contests. Many athletes physically grab, slam into, and yell encouragement at teammates, while also expressing a great deal of intense emotion towards competitors, *occasionally* using language you don't hear in church! While audiences may find such behavior entertaining, performance psychology research clearly indicates that fever-pitched emotionality, and the words and actions that accompany it, interfere with rather than enhance carrying out complex physical and mental tasks.

Fishing, especially competitive fishing, is a technically complex, intellectually intricate, and physically demanding sport. If you make bad decisions, lose focus, or execute carelessly, even for a moment, you may miss fish, perhaps *the fish* that would have won the tournament.

Unbridled expressions of raw passion diminish your capacity to concentrate, focus on, and precisely execute complex tasks like skipping lures under boat docks, reading electronics, and maneuvering your boat. Additionally, people who are emotionally intense spend a lot of time being, well, emotionally intense! At a practical level, prolonged emotional episodes during a tournament can waste valuable fishing time. Especially on days when the fish bite only briefly, you want to keep fishing rather than celebrate, or act upset, don't you?

I was paired with Roland Martin in a pro-am tournament in which six inches of rain fell in one day. (That was when I discovered, by the way, that 75 mph in a bass boat in torrential rain means getting soaked to skin, even if you are wearing *two* rain suits!) Fishing was difficult, and for several hours neither of us had had a bite. Late in the day on an unremarkable bank we hooked, between us, six fish in about eight casts. Then suddenly, just as fast as it started, the bite was over. You have most likely had a similar experience. An emotional episode at a time like this could cause an angler to miss the one decent fishing flurry of the day.

Intense emotional episodes will also eventually wear you out. Think back on prolonged stressful events you have experienced and recall how exhausted or drained you felt afterward. Monitoring your emotional intensity, especially during fishing tournaments, is essentially equivalent to keeping an eye on the gas gauge. You need to have enough emotional energy (and outboard motor fuel!) to last the entire day. Of course, people who "let it all hang out" certainly can still be successful. Just remember, such individuals succeed *in spite of,* not because of this facet of their personality, regardless of what they may believe or say.

If you want to prove this to yourself, try an experiment other top anglers have used. Tie a jig on your pitchin' stick and get a tin pie plate, then head to the back yard. Put the plate at a distance (not too close, not too far) where you can drop your jig on it five times out of six. Now, with the help of someone who can keep a secret, think of a subject that really makes you upset and go off on a large-scale two minute rant. See if you can bring yourself to scream and yell, wave your arms around, pump your fist, or otherwise imitate some guy making a complete fool out of himself. After you have imitated Mr. Wild Man, pick up your rod and see if *even one* of the next six pitches hits the plate!

Now, don't get me wrong. I don't mean to be negatively judgmental of people who get a little excited now and then. Why, the author of this book has been known to express a strong emotion or two over the years! Once, he got genuinely carried away. Okay, more than once! However, no matter who you are, excessive emotionality has associated risks and downsides you need to appreciate.

Most importantly, being "In The Zone" is incompatible with anger, worry, and frustration. Most of us experience a wide range of emotions, some of which can be intense, in any given week. However, if you or one of your fishing colleagues experience frequent and/or intense episodes of irritation, aggravation, or anger, you would do well to pay attention to this phenomena. One pro I worked with came to our sixth or seventh session and said, "You know Doc, I just get angry too easily and too often. It's a bunch of little stuff that triggers my reactions, but I know it throws me off". We talked this through, and came up with some different strategies on how he could handle the circumstances that he previously found irritating. Certainly containing frustrated, irritable reactions is no guarantee that you will wind up "In the Zone", though being in an angry mood is a sure way to *keep* from getting there!

Insufficient Intensity

This phenomenon doesn't occur often, but it's frequent enough for comment. There are some individuals, and also individuals in certain circumstances, who have difficulty getting motivated for a particular day or event. A certain level of inner drive, passion, and commitment whether enthusiastically or quietly expressed, is necessary to be competitive. The extraordinarily passive, unmotivated, low-energy individual will have difficulty tackling difficult tasks. If you suffer from this low-energy, low-passion syndrome, you may be reluctant to put in extra practice time, or you may find yourself less than fully alert. Perhaps your mind wanders where and when it shouldn't.

One professional I worked with was preoccupied with a failing family business. For several sessions he talked at great length about a successful three-generation company being swept away by new technology and a diminishing customer base. He spent so much time and energy fretting about the business, and calling home to check on day-to-day operations, that he was unable to muster much enthusiasm for tournament days, let alone for practice time. It took him some time to work through this but eventually he was able to do a better job of compartmentalizing his thoughts and feelings about the business so that he could rekindle his passion for fishing.

Putting Yourself "In The Zone"

As suggested, it is beyond current knowledge and expertise to offer precise suggestions or plans that will put you "In The Zone" on a regular basis. However, here are some predisposing factors you can cultivate:

- Challenge: In most instances, top performers experience being "In The Zone" when they have pushed themselves harder and/or farther than they thought possible. I do not recommend that you take reckless risks. However, "Play It Safe" rarely carries competitors into the flow of optimum intensity. Setting aggressive immediate as well as short-term goals can help keep your personal challenges front and center, a place where "In The Zone" can flourish.

92

- Focused Concentration: Being "In The Zone" is directly related to the ability to focus specifically and fully on the task at hand. Fishermen frequently describe the intensity of concentration when their jig, plastic worm, or crank bait hits the water and they almost *experience* the bait as it comes back to them.   They describe being oblivious to the rod, the reel, and the line. More than one angler has told me, quietly and somewhat sheepishly, something to the effect of "You know Doc, this sounds stupid but that day when I was really *there*, it felt like I was down in the water with my plastic worm. I could sense it and feel it moving up and down off the bottom; it was almost like I was there with it crawling over each twig and branch on the trees I was fishing". This intense concentration, while difficult to attain, is nevertheless frequently associated with optimal intensity.

- Detachment: Key performers frequently comment that being "In The Zone" includes a distinctly different attitude toward the final outcome from what they usually experience. One pro angler put it this way, "Most of the time I'm acutely aware of how much weight I have and how much I need to win. If I'm fishing near other guys, I catch myself watching them, trying to determine if they are catching more or bigger fish than I am. However, when I'm "In The Zone", it's like there's no one on the lake but me. It's a very intense experience at one level, though in another way it seems as though the competition, the trophy, the money, none of that really matters."

- Acceptance: Top competitors also describe the experience of noticing but being in harmony with their circumstances when the "In The Zone" experience occurs. One guy told me, "On most days I think consciously about how the wind, rain, current, or lake level might be helping or hurting my fishing. On those rare instances when I feel everything flow together, I still notice those things though I don't have the same judgments about them. Whatever is happening at the moment feels like *exactly what should be happening*. I don't feel like I am wrestling with the wind or resisting the rain, things I might feel on a typical day". As you cultivate this feeling of inner harmony with your natural surroundings it appears the experience of optimal intensity, or *Flow*, or being "In The Zone" is likely to occur more often.

REGULAR GUY TIP

Reaching your Optimal Intensity, or getting "In The Zone" may seem far-fetched, but it's not, really. Think of it this way. Are you the kind of guy who is bright-eyed and bushy-tailed, ready to go first thing in the morning, or are you someone who eases into the day and hits his fishing stride later in the day, say mid-afternoon? Knowing when you are naturally at your optimal level of emotional energy is a good starting point on your way to being "In The Zone"!!

CHAPTER **18**

Confidence:
What Is It Really? And How Do I Get More?

Conventional wisdom tells us that confidence primarily comes from being successful. In fishing, this translates to: "The more fish I catch, the more confident I feel." Too many anglers, including more than a few competitive fishermen, believe that confidence *only* comes from catching a lot of fish, and big ones! Certainly a heavy stringer, or a high finish in a tournament can give your *fishing* confidence a lift. At the same time, genuine self-confidence rests on many different things, only one of which is how you fished today.

Self-Confidence vs. Performance Confidence

Clearly, being a successful, confident angler is important to anyone reading this book. However, it's crucial to differentiate between the confidence you have in yourself as a person, and the confidence you have about a particular skill or talent, such as fishing.

Basic self-confidence or self-esteem is based on who you are. This includes your values, your talents and abilities, your priorities and commitments, and the several roles you play in life, a successful angler being one of these. As you have seen, many of the exercises in **The Psychology of Exceptional Fishing** have been aimed at increasing self-awareness and self-understanding. Confident individuals have a realistic, accurate, and fairly comprehensive understanding of themselves. Additionally, confident people tend to be tolerant, accepting, and comfortable with who and what they are. Okay, so you're not perfect; but you are who you are, and you would do well to appreciate yourself as best you can. As you read in **Chapter 3**, and elsewhere, self-acceptance is a key performance psychology concept.

Confident people not only value themselves, they also feel valued by others. None of us were born confident. However, with sufficient love, acceptance, and encouragement, first from your immediate family, and then later from peers and role models, true confidence eventually developed. You went from being dependent on, yet confident in the people around you to being confident about yourself and your own ability to make your way in the world.

This last dimension represents what psychologists call self-efficacy, which means the capacity to adapt to and deal with circumstances, both good and bad, as they arise. Confidence allows you to recognize and overcome the fears, anxieties, and difficulties life deals out, including things you have not previously experienced.

For example, given the challenge, most of you could confidently find your way to Flin Flon, Manitoba, Canada even though you've probably never been there. Obviously you can't be confident about retracing your steps! However, you are sure of your ability to make plane reservations, buy bus tickets, arrange rental cars, and read roadmaps, these skills allowing you to confidently make your way to Flin Flon!

To extend this analogy to fishing, if you are confident about your boat driving ability, your sonar reading capabilities, and your understanding of midsummer fish behavior on natural lakes, and if you know how to work a Carolina rig or a deep crankbait, you can probably come in July or August to the lakes I fish in Minnesota and catch them.

Oh, sorry! You guys who are pro anglers already did that! If you pay attention to competitive fishing history, you probably know that both the *FLW* and the *Bassmasters* brought their tournament trails to Lake Minnetonka, here on the outskirts of Minneapolis. In both settings, professional anglers confident of their midsummer fishing skills, who had never seen the lake prior to these events, essentially "wore 'em out"!

Ultimately, solid self-confidence rests on being able to put several elements together. If you have people around you who value and believe in you, if you know and accept yourself, and if you have a sense of being able to deal adaptively with whatever comes along, you can expect to be a confident, self-assured person.

Building Confidence

In **Chapter 2**, you found exercises designed to help improve your self-understanding. In **Chapter 5** you made a catalogue of your internal resources, skills about which you are currently confident. **Exercise 23** uses a different approach to self-awareness.

Borrowing liberally from **Exercises 1, 6,** and **9,** use the table below to paint another picture of who you are. In the first column under traits, write down the main personality characteristics people would use to describe you. In the second column write down the different roles you play such as successful angler, loyal friend, and so forth. In the third column write down the principles you believe in that guide your life. Things like thoughtfulness, generosity, and such would go in this column.

As with other self-discovery exercises, take some time to make this process complete, and use other people to help you out. Your two best buddies and your closest relative can help you identify or perhaps emphasize traits, roles, and values that are important to you. Once you have finished this list, read it through slowly and deliberately. Let me add an interesting twist, one I think you'll enjoy.

Having read through your list (and checked it for accuracy!), find a quiet place where you can be alone, and read your list out loud. Many people have indicated that completing the written part of this exercise was a positive experience. However, the process of reading what they wrote *out loud* adds an entirely different dimension. Said one pro, "You know, it was a fun list to create. But then I started to say these things out loud. It went from an intellectual exercise to being an intense personal experience. When I finished, I sat back and said 'Yeah, this really *is* who I am.' It made a big difference in how I think about myself."

I encourage you to do **Exercise 23** first, though it might be easier to do this next one, **Exercise 24,** as a kind of warm up. If you've been fishing for any length of time, and I suspect you have, there are some facets of fishing about which you already feel pretty confident. You don't have to worry, for example, about catching crappies in April on your home lake, because you know just where to go, what to do, and how to catch them.

Similarly, you might be quite sure of your ability to go to most any highland reservoir and catch largemouth or smallmouth off deep ledges in the summer with crankbaits, football jigs, or Carolina rigs. Well, good for you. **Exercise 24** will help you expand on the skill and technique confidence you already have.

Exercise 23: SELF-AWARENESS

Traits	Roles	Values
e.g. Cheerful, helpful, moody, determined	e.g. Father, son, breadwinner, angler	e.g. Honesty, trust, openness, spontaneity

In terms of building fishing confidence, **Exercise 24** uses three categories: things you're very confident about, things where you are moderately confident, and dimensions where your confidence could use a boost. This really is a fun exercise, in case you haven't done it before. Most of the anglers I have worked with tell me this is the exercise they enjoy most. Here, just finish each sentence stem below.

Exercise 24: FISHING CONFIDENCE

I am very good at:

I am very good at:

I am very good at:

I am very good at:

I am very good at:

I am very good at:

I am very good at:

I am very good at:

I am very good at:

I am very good at:

I am very good at:

I am very good at:

I am very good at:

I am very good at:

I am very good at:

I am usually pretty good at:

I am usually pretty good at:

I am usually pretty good at:

I am usually pretty good at:

I am usually pretty good at:

I am usually pretty good at:

I am usually pretty good at:

I am usually pretty good at:

I am usually pretty good at:

I am usually pretty good at:

I need to be better at:

I need to be better at:

I need to be better at:

I need to be better at:

I need to be better at:

I need to be better at:

I need to be better at:

I need to be better at:

I need to be better at:

I need to be better at:

Exercise 24 does several things for you. First, it broadens and expands your sense of confidence. Instead of having your fishing confidence rest on only a few dimensions, completing this exercise will give you a more comprehensive picture of those fishing skills where you are very, or usually skilled. Secondly this exercise can serve as a reference point on those days when you are feeling discouraged or disappointed. When you have a lousy day on the water, it's easy to say what I have heard many pros say, "After today, I just don't feel very confident".

What you really mean is, you feel discouraged, frustrated, or disappointed about not catching fish *that day, under those circumstances*. It's important to not equate your immediate feelings about the moment with your overall confidence, however. Remember, what you think influences what you say; at the same time, what you say also influences what you think! In other words, if you *tell* yourself you're not confident, you can easily start to *feel* less confident. Instead, when you have a bad day fishing go ahead and say you're frustrated, upset, or whatever; just don't say you're not confident!

Several anglers have told me this particular exercise has helped them maintain their confidence following a less-then-perfect fishing day. In addition to the exercise above, some competitive anglers carry with them lucky lures, a list of tournament victories, or photos of dandy fish. Having to such items around (or referring to the exercise above) can help maintain your confidence, even when the fish don't cooperate. The lesson here is your self-confidence can remain solid and steady, even though your emotions, your day-to-day performance, and the circumstances around you might change substantially.

Confidence Is Overrated!

At the risk of contradicting everything I just said, let me offer a caution against overemphasizing the importance of confidence. It is this: You don't have to *feel* confident to be successful. Repeatedly I hear tournament anglers say, "I can't win until I feel more confident." This is a huge mistake, because it's just not true! There are a zillion examples I can think of, and probably two zillion more that you know to illustrate this.

When Larry Nixon won that tournament on Lake Wheeler a few years back, do you think it was with supreme confidence that on the last day he got half way to the spot where he had been catching them all week, stopped, turned his boat around, and went to an entirely new area?

Or, what do you suppose Jim Moynagh's confidence was prior to catching fish on the last day of his FLW victory on Lake Minnetonka knowing, as he said at the weigh-in, "They weren't there in practice."?

Or put yourself in Jay Yelas's shoes immediately prior to what is perhaps the most televised single cast in bass fishing history, the one he made into the wake of that crazy pontoon boat on Lay Lake not so long ago, when he caught the biggest fish of the *Bassmaster's Classic,* which he won. Could you, or Jay, or really anyone be confident of *that* cast?

In all three instances, successful anglers didn't *have to* be confident about an area, a spot or even a specific cast. They won anyway! Persistence, tenacity, and "doing what needs to be done" can carry you even when you don't have all the confidence you want, or think you need!

And finally, if all else fails and you need a shot of confidence, borrow some from someone else! The first check I ever cashed in a tournament came this way. It was close to weigh-in time, and we needed one more good fish. I was completely out of ideas, so I sat down in the back of Bradley's boat and said to myself, "What would Denny Brauer do?" Then I reached into my tackle bag for a black-and-blue jig/craw and pitched into the thickest stuff I could reach. It was Denny's confidence, not mine, in that black-and-blue bait that allowed me to catch the final 3-pounder that put us in the money.

REGULAR GUY TIP

If you don't really want to do those big long exercises, get a piece of paper and a pencil and write down as many of the fishing things you're good at that come to mind. Don't show your list to anybody, just fold it up, stick it in your tackle box, and read it on those days when you're not sure what to do. And let me know if it helps!

CHAPTER 19

A Psychological Tackle Box:
Mental Lures for All Seasons!

At this point, you have a great deal of information about how psychological dimensions can improve fishing success. You know more about yourself, you've developed some plans and systems, and you have tried several mental techniques that research and personal experience say are useful. However, in some respects, you are a lot like the lucky angler who has just finished spending a fifteen hundred dollar gift certificate at *Bass Pro Shops*. You have a large selection of useful stuff that *could* help you catch more fish, though to use it efficiently you need to get it organized. What you really need is to create a **Psychological Tackle Box!**

As you know, there are several ways to organize your fishing tackle. Similarly, there are many different ways to organize and use psychological techniques as. Let me propose a system that has worked for athletes in many other sports.

A) Ongoing Mental Exercises

Based on what you have read so far, you have probably come to the conclusion that at least *some* performance psychology techniques could be helpful on an ongoing basis, and you are exactly right. Relaxation exercises, concentration skills, mental rehearsal techniques, and visualization are examples of practices can be useful this week, next week, and every week. Research studies tell us these techniques practiced on a regular basis will show significant cumulative benefits as well. The more you practice a particular technique, the stronger your mastery of that technique will become.

A good **Psychological Tackle Box** includes at least ten minutes three or four times a week to practice your chosen mental exercises. Touring professionals tell me there are two timeframes in particular that lend themselves well to mental exercises. One is in the evening after they have returned to their campground, home, or motel room after a day on the water. Finding a quiet spot, turning off the radio or the television, and doing a series of relaxation, concentration, and/or visualization exercises helps them feel calmer and more at ease. Using psychological techniques in the evening also helps them focus on what is most important *that day*.

Additionally, pros describe early morning, pre-takeoff time as conducive to using mental exercises. Rehearsing your game plan, visualizing success experiences, and using focusing and concentration exercises can help calm, or eliminate, the jittery feelings that occur prior to a big fishing day.

B) Pre-Competition Routine

It is especially critical for you to put together a specific set of techniques to use prior to practice and competition days. You don't need me to tell you how important it is to be at the top of your game, *physically and mentally,* before and during tournaments. Depending on your unique circumstances, you may have a special visual picture to focus on the morning of, or the night before each competition day. Perhaps a favorite set of words or affirmations, or a particular song or prayer will work especially well for you. A pre-competition routine that includes psychological strengthening techniques can help put you in an optimal frame of mind.

C) Annual Review

Regardless of the specific subset of techniques and exercises you adopt for yourself, it is very important to review them on a regular basis. Some pros like to do an annual review soon after the current fishing season ends in order to record or chronicle successes as well as failures while they are still fresh memories. Others like to wait awhile and spend time thinking about what went well and what didn't before making summary notes. However, at a minimum, your **Psychological Tackle Box** needs to be cleaned out and resorted once a year, just like your real tackle box!

However, if you are serious about fishing, you don't just do your tackle once a year. Similarly, your **Psychological Tackle Box** also needs regular attention. Many top-shelf athletes do a quarterly review, a timeframe I recommend as well. On your calendar, give yourself an hour every three months to do a mental review. These quarterly checkpoints, especially if they involve discussions with fellow anglers, can serve to reinvigorate your commitment to your mental strengthening techniques. Quarterly reviews of your **Psychological Tackle Box** allow you to add, delete, or modify items as necessary. In order to best illustrate how this works, let me tell you two stories about two different individuals and the path each took to creating and using a **Psychological Tackle Box**.

Joe

Joe was in his mid-twenties when I met him. He had been in a bass club for a few years and had fished occasionally in small money events. Joe watched the Saturday morning fishing shows, and his dream was to join a pro tour within five years. However, Joe was plagued by inconsistent fishing success. He also openly described the wide and erratic mood swings he experienced during the course of his fishing season. After catching a nice fish or two, he would be, in his words, "high as a kite". At such times he talked endlessly with friends about his big catch. For a few days, at least, he would feel ready to quit his day job, dip into his savings account, and lay out the entry fees the pro tournaments demanded.

However, his enthusiasm was fairly predictably crushed the following week when Joe was unable to repeat his success. At such times, his discouragement and aggravation were such that he thought of abandoning his fishing dreams altogether. Joe initially came to me for help because he thought a sport psychologist could help him be more consistent in catching fish. He eventually came to appreciate that a more consistent mood and more dependable psychological functioning might be important prerequisites to better fishing!

Joe was a determined, if not consistently committed student. He went through the exercises outlined in **Chapters 1-5**, clarifying his commitments and solidifying his priorities. He got his fishing colleagues to help him figure out the practical fishing skills he was good at, and they also told him where he needed to improve. Joe was particularly excited about doing his personal inventory. He came to realize that his extreme emotionality was both his best psychological asset and a primary liability. Initially, Joe's goal was to be "up" all the time, though as we worked together he began to appreciate that this was probably not possible, or even desirable. He talked about his excitable, passionate episodes as enjoyable, yet he could also admit that at such times he was typically going in forty different directions at once. At his worst, he was scattered, unfocused, and erratic, and not at all consistent about important matters like equipment maintenance, or following through on promises to his fishing club pals.

In his excited moments, he fished with unbridled enthusiasm and passion. He could make more casts per hour than anyone. Nevertheless, when he was "cranked up" he was also inclined to make foolish mistakes, like forgetting to buy his fishing license in a neighboring state, leaving an important piece of tackle in his truck, or on several occasions, trying to put his boat on plane without having pulled up the trolling motor! In reviewing the pluses and minuses associated with his energetic, optimistic episodes, Joe was somewhat reluctant to change. He didn't want to let go of being "up". The turning point came for him early one tournament morning when he filled both his truck and boat with gas and then drove off without paying! Joe described the embarrassment of realizing this mistake later in the morning. With help from his co-angler, he called the station on his cell phone and told them he realized what he had done. The station manager, who was also a local deputy sheriff, had just come on duty and was getting the report from his station attendant when Joe called. Fortunately, a legal crisis was averted!

Following this humbling experience, Joe came to see he needed to level off some of the peaks and valleys in his emotional experience. A series of refocusing and relaxation exercises helped Joe internally. He also "recruited" a couple members of his bass club, also excitable guys, to use as sounding boards. Both when he started to rev up, and when he became discouraged, his "posse" as he called them, was able to help him maintain a bit more of an even keel.

Because of his excitable nature, Joe especially benefited from the suggestions outlined in **Chapter 9** on routines and rituals. Once he created a specific pre-fishing trip routine, Joe found that even when he was excited he made fewer careless mistakes and thereby saved himself numerous headaches. He also identified some shirts and hats that were associated with not only fishing well, but with being emotionally steady!

Not surprisingly, Joe had little difficulty getting "psyched up" for the start of most practice or competition days. However, he did have difficulty maintaining his positive attitude if he did not experience early fishing success. After a fishless hour or two, Joe's mood began to slide noticeably. To counter this, he tried to add visualization techniques and optimal intensity exercises to his **Psychological Tackle Box** to help maintain appropriate levels of enthusiasm during competitive events.

Perhaps most significantly, Joe was able to develop an end-of-the-day routine to keep his emotions from spiraling out of control, either upward or downward. This was something of a challenge, as Joe found great satisfaction in distributing as well as consuming "cheer" from his cooler, especially after a successful trip! However, Joe did have some success displaying a more moderate reaction on his best fishing days. He was also able to come across as *slightly* more humble and tactful in response to people who did not do as well as he did. During the course of the first season we worked together, one of Joe's most telling remarks was how members of his club seemed to have more respect for him in direct proportion to his ability to contain his extreme emotional reactions.

Additionally, Joe worked to bridge the gap between his current fishing situation and his obviously aggressive five-year objective. Since he had been on construction crews during high school and college, Joe was able to appreciate the value of having a solid blue-print and a realistic estimate of costs before deciding to build something, like a garage. In Joe's case, he was able to interview other top-level fishermen in his area, create yearly objectives for the next four years, and build in specific, measurable outcome criteria to help him determine whether he was successfully moving toward his long-range goal to be a full-time professional angler.

I would *like* to tell you that Joe was able to harness his intense emotionality, build on his previous fishing successes, and realize his long-term objective. However, about two years after we met, Joe got a job in another state and moved, so I lost track of him. During our time together, however, Joe was able to put together his own **Psychological Tackle Box**, one that matched his temperament and his particular fishing needs. He did move from 14th to 6th in his bass club in the time we worked together. And his Christmas card this year says he is not yet ready to change or give up his long-range goal!

Ralph

I was somewhat surprised to get a call from Ralph. While not a top professional, he had fished national events for a number of years and was widely regarded as a good hook. Early middle-aged, Ralph had been highly successful in local settings, and he had won a couple of boats in individual and team events at a regional level. He joined the pro ranks at a time when, as he put it, "there wasn't nearly as much competition as there is now." However, he didn't experience the same level of success in the top echelons of fishing that he had previously, and there was clearly a discouraged tone in his voice when he reached out for help.

Ralph went through the standard self-assessment exercises, clarifying his priorities and establishing his commitments. Ralph's work was impressive here as he was clearly an introspective, thoughtful individual. Obviously he had already put a fair amount of time into making sure his competitive fishing career was adaptively aligned with the important people and events in his life. Ralph was very invested in community service work, for example, and his commitments here were impressive.

However, as Ralph completed the practical skills and self-awareness exercises, it became clear that he did not hold himself or his fishing skills in particularly high regard. He was modest, to the point of being self-effacing, when cataloguing his internal resources. Ralph's list of influential people and events also reflected a somewhat discouraging tone. Many people had told him that making a living at fishing was futile, unrealistic, or stupid. Ralph did identify one high school coach who was universally supportive and encouraging. Even though Ralph was undersized and unlikely to be a starter, this coach encouraged him to stay with the team and see what developed. With an uncharacteristically bright expression, Ralph described how his teammates accepted him and admired his continued hard work and dedication in the face of obvious physical limitations. Ralph also talked about how this coach focused a lot on intangibles like dedication, heart, and character, regardless of whether the team was winning handily or getting trounced.

Ralph, as you may have guessed, was already good at planning and organizing things. He was highly attentive to detail, and so the keeping track techniques, as well as the planning and goal-setting exercises were easy and straightforward for him. He already had several adaptive routines that he used, and he had the type of time management skills that others would do well to imitate. However, Ralph was also something of a loner, and he admitted that he relied extensively, often exclusively, on himself to evaluate his techniques and make needed changes. He pushed himself to do his best. Nevertheless, he was quick, sometimes too quick, to criticize less-than-perfect performance.

When it came to building a **Psychological Tackle Box** with Ralph there was a clear need for him to expand his sense of professional competence. Ralph found the exercises on confidence-building particularly valuable, and he was pleasantly surprised at the number of individual fishing skills in which he felt reasonably confident. He was also able to successfully recreate a number of positive visual images that slowly but surely began to further expand his sense of mastery.

Mental rehearsal techniques were particularly valuable for Ralph. He came to realize that while he often reviewed his past performance, what he *usually did* was repeatedly replay his mistakes. In the office setting, Ralph was able to see how he could easily erase almost all of his positive feelings by dwelling on what he had done wrong! He began exploring the technique of mentally correcting past mistakes that had previously plagued him. Ralph was visibly encouraged by some immediate success here.

A key moment for Ralph occurred when we talked about re-contacting his supportive high school coach. Ralph described in some detail how he had, in fact, kept in touch with this individual for several years after graduation. Sadly, this man had died about ten years previously, leaving a void for Ralph that our discussions revealed was still there. I asked Ralph about individuals in his life currently who might play a similar role for him, and at first he seemed stumped and discouraged.

However, as Ralph began to talk more about the people on the periphery of his fishing circles, he identified a few possibilities, one being a representative from his primary sponsor, and another being an elder in his church. I encouraged Ralph to explore these relationships—subtly at first and then more directly. As things developed with these two individuals, Ralph began to appreciate more clearly than before the importance of individuals who were unequivocally supportive. Ralph began to understand the "no man is an island" concept, and he began to see how in some ways he had retreated into himself more than was beneficial since the death of his mentor many years ago.

Ralph also made a conscious effort to focus more on his practical strengths. Using his own observations, as well as feedback from trusted colleagues, Ralph began to upgrade his self-assessment in a variety of domains. This gave him reason for greater optimism when looking at the upcoming tournament season.

Like a lot of individuals, Ralph was somewhat leery about coming to see the "fishing shrink," and the truth of the matter is we only had a handful of sessions together. However, over the past three seasons he has strengthened his angler of the year point standings, and indirect sources confirm what his infrequent emails indicate, that his self-confidence is stronger and his professional self-image is more positive than it was.

REGULAR GUY TIP

Whether or not you realize it, you *already have* a **Psychological Tackle Box**! Yup, that's right, you do! Even today you use psychological mechanisms like rationalization to deal with stress ("Yeah, I know I didn't catch any fish last time, but neither did anybody else! ") and regardless of the nicknames you have for each other, the guys you fish with are your social support network! So why not add one more psychological technique like visualization or mental rehearsal to your **Psychological Tackle Box**....one more lure or technique can only help, right?

CHAPTER 20

Public Speaking:
Put Your Best Foot Forward, Not in Your Mouth!

Historically, anglers have been pretty tightlipped about their fishing secrets. When it comes to hot spots and magic lures, talented fishermen say nothing, or lie. And for good reason. You don't have to go back too many generations to appreciate the survival value of keeping your mouth shut about places and methods that provided dinner! Like most people, you are probably genetically hardwired to remain silent when the topic of secret fishing spots comes up!

But then, somebody invented the Supermarket, and pretty soon people weren't just fishing for food anymore, they were fishing for fun! Well, what's fun for one ought to be even more fun for two or three or four! Once anglers started to congregate, somebody eventually said, "Say, as long as we're all here, let's have a contest!" Welcome to the Age of Tournament Fishing!

At the first competitive events, successful anglers shuffled politely through the crowd and quietly collected their money. If there was any kind of conversation with the person running the tournament it mostly involved staring at your feet while saying something profound like," I'm sure glad to be here", before nervously slinking away. There wasn't much talk back then because, well, anglers didn't go to contests to give speeches, they went to fish! But saying a few words, especially if you won, wasn't all that bad, because the only people in the crowd were the other guys in the fishing contest!

Why, oh why, couldn't they just leave well enough alone? Well, they just couldn't, that's all, and the next thing that happened was tournament organizers invited the whole dang town out to watch the weigh-ins! The worst part of *that* was the people all stood around and stared while you were asked questions you *really* didn't want to answer like, "Where'd you catch your fish?", and "What color lure did you use?" ("What *is* that fool thinkin'," you said to yourself. "There's another contest here in three weeks! I'd have to be *crazy* to tell these people how I caught my fish.")

'Course, then it went from bad to worse, because pretty soon they built a stage, and a big tall one, too! Then along came more and bigger sponsors who paid the tournament entry fees, and that was good, but now your sponsor wanted you to get up there on that platform and show off that fancy shirt with all the logos on it, and you had to do that even when you only caught two little dinks, or nothing at all! But the real kicker was when they started puttin' it all on TV! Television interviews made *everybody* nervous, and that was *real* obvious a few weeks later when you watched yourself on the show!

Okay, so maybe I exaggerated a little bit, but the truth is professional, semi-pro, and amateur anglers often struggle with the pressures of public speaking. However, let me reassure you it is not easy for *most* people to speak in front of a group, especially a large group. Since this is such a universal difficulty, many techniques and strategies have been created to make public speaking easier. Full coverage of public speaking is beyond the scope of this book. However, here a few ideas that have helped others.

This discussion begins with the assertion that effective public speaking and presentation skills are more often learned than inherited. Some of the best public speakers started out tentative, awkward, and ineffective. So, don't despair if you currently struggle with less than perfect public speaking skills. They can be acquired and mastered!

What *exactly* is the problem?

As other discussions in this book have illustrated, I believe it is best to dissect and understand a situation before trying to change it. So, as a first step, take some time to think about what part of public speaking is most challenging. Some people say that addressing a crowd isn't too bad if they are prepared, whereas trying to say something clever on the spur of the moment is stressful. Other people find that looking out on an audience causes them to get tongue-tied and freeze up, or *worry* about getting tongue-tied and freezing up. One pro told me "If I just stay focused on the tournament director and only talk to him I'm fine. It's when I try to face the crowd that my voice disappears." Many people have admitted they are most apprehensive about being asked questions they did not expect. Let's talk about this latter situation first.

Unexpected Questions

When you think about it, there really aren't *that* many different types of questions that tournament directors can ask on the weigh-in stand. So, talk with your fishing buddies about commonly asked questions and see if you can develop two or three ways to respond to each one.

A couple guys I know from a neighboring state fished money tournaments in Minnesota. Since they weren't very talented public speakers, they would spend their drive time to and from tournaments trying to anticipate what questions might come up and possible ways to respond to them. When I met them they were already smooth presenters, and it was not at all obvious that their public speaking skills had been rehearsed and revised over the course of many miles.

One particularly helpful technique a few anglers have used is to devise both a serious and a humorous response to tournament-related questions. Some of the comments I have heard are laugh-out-loud ridiculous! I even know one guy who is just waiting to be asked a certain question because of the witty reply he is set to deliver!

Brief is Better, and Other Tips

One of the biggest mistakes anglers who struggle with public speaking make is trying to say too much. The tournament director asks how deep the fish were, and the guy in the fancy shirt tries to describe the entire contour map of the lake. Not good! Interviewers want an answer, that's for sure, but in most cases they don't want a speech. Typically two or three sentences are enough.

Also, develop a few standard responses in case questions do catch you off guard. For example, if the interviewer asks a question you can't or don't want to answer, just smile politely and say something like "You're guess is as good as mine" or "I don't think I can help you there, Bill."

As mentioned, making eye contact with the audience can be stressful for some people, so don't do that. Instead, look at the interviewer and talk directly to that person. And try to ignore the camera. You will look just fine on television if you are making direct eye contact with the person asking the questions. However, if looking a person straight in the eye is distracting, as it is for some of us, focus on the interviewer's ear or hat. Just keep your chin up and don't let yourself look at the floor. Also, be sure to take off your sunglasses. And if it's not too much work, try to smile when you're talking; but don't force it.

Finally, if through no fault of your own you wind up facing the audience, do what singers and actors do: pick a spot in the back of the room *above everyone's head* and lock in on that spot while you talk. It will make your public speaking experience a whole lot easier.

As you become more successful, there will be an increasing number of opportunities to do public presentations. While this may seem nerve-racking, in actuality, it is exactly what you want. With public speaking, the more you practice, the better you will get. If you are asked to do seminars or demonstrations, start by writing out exactly what you want to say. It may seem awkward at first, but there is nothing wrong with using notes or file cards. Lots of people read from scripts, including the president! Once you have given the same talk a few times, you will refer to your written notes less and less often.

You can also build public speaking confidence in the privacy of your own home. For many, rehearsing in front of a mirror develops comfort and confidence that transfers over when they step in front of an audience. Consider doing this in advance of your next public speaking event.

Exercise 25: Presentation Practice

Put on the same tournament shirt you wear when you give presentations, and stand in front of a mirror. Begin by monitoring your posture. Stand tall, look straight ahead, and hold your script comfortably with both hands. Then read your script out loud, taking care to speak slowly and clearly. Nervous public speakers either talk too softly or too quickly. Experiment with tone of voice, word emphasis, and the volume of your speech.

Once you are familiar and comfortable with the script, try saying a few words straight into the mirror before referring back your notes. Practice walking around while you talk, and use hand gestures, trying different movements to see what feels comfortable. Even going through your presentation as few as three or four times will make a significant difference in how confident you feel when you stand before a crowd. Remember, smile if you can, and keep the volume up, the speed down.

Use Available Resources

There are numerous books, seminars, videos and self-help groups available for those who want to seriously tackle public speaking. One organization I unequivocally recommend is *Toastmasters*. This group conducts weekly meetings in every town, and in large cities there are numerous groups to choose from. It is, in my experience, a consistently supportive, instructional, low-pressure setting in which to experiment with different public speaking and presentation techniques.

Additionally, consider borrowing or renting a movie camera and videotaping yourself. What you *think* you look and sound like *is not*, I promise, what you will find when you play back the tape! The camera tells it like it is, and yet it provides immediate feedback. I think you will be pleasantly surprised to find what an hour or two of experimenting with and watching different presentation styles can do for you.

Also, speech coaches are both popular and helpful. A good speech coach will give you nearly as much accurate information as a camera, with the added advantage that a speech coach can offer suggestions and *demonstrate* different ways of speaking.

Observe an Expert

To be sure, you wouldn't be the first person to benefit from watching a video or two of an excellent speaker. Good speakers take on and then project a public persona which is quite a lot like what you do when you wear your tournament fishing shirt! With that shirt on, you're not just Ralph or Joe anymore; instead, you become a representative, an ambassador for the organizations who sponsor you. With a little practice, however, you can create a professional presence that includes effective public speaking and solid presentation skills.

As a final thought, in my experience most tournament anglers speak from the heart in a sincere, genuine, down-to-earth manner. In many cases, just being yourself is good enough, though practicing your presentation skills is a surefire path to success!

REGULAR GUY TIP

Your buddies may have told you that public speaking skills aren't all that important, that what matters is catching fish. With all due respect to your pals, that's just not true. If you have, or want sponsors, you need to understand what they want from you, and part of what they want is somebody who presents their products and their company in a positive way. Think of your own experience; when you go into a store, you want clerks who can effectively communicate with you. Part of communicating for your sponsors includes good public presentation skills. However, you may be independently wealthy and so you don't need sponsors; in that case, forget this public speaking stuff!

CHAPTER **21**

Conflict Resolution:
How to Get What You Want Without a Fight!

Daffodils have always been a beautiful and powerful sign that spring is here to stay. They rise confidently out of the ground at a time of year when other plants are still timidly hidden away. We saw several of those delicate yet determined buds on that March morning in St. Louis many years ago. It was Friday, and some graduate students were about to meet with their Director of Clinical Training. Near the end of our session, the director's phone range and he took the call. After listening for several long moments, a sly smile spread across his face and he said, "No, I don't think so. Thanks for calling." Almost in unison, the seven of us asked, "What was that?" Turns out the caller was a local radio talk show host looking for a psychologist from the University of Missouri-St. Louis to be on his program and answer calls addressing the topic "Why Don't People Get Along?" We were young and foolish, and therefore shocked that our mentor had turned down such an opportunity to spread the "Good News of Psychology" to the oh-so-needy public. Later, we realized what we had seen, a perfect illustration of "How do you respond to a question that is impossible to answer? You *don't* respond!" With that in mind, I would like to beg the late Dr. Louis Sherman's forgiveness for this feeble attempt to address a topic as old and complex as human nature itself.

In the following paragraphs I am going to offer a few thoughts about conflict resolution in the context of competitive fishing, specifically dealing with boat partners or fellow anglers with whom you interact frequently. However, **do not** take these techniques home and try them on members of your family! Most assuredly, do not march into the next Fourth of July family picnic or Thanksgiving dinner and tell your third cousins twice removed about the techniques you have learned that, if they would only use them, could resolve their long-standing differences!

In competitive fishing circles, there is near unanimous agreement that a hostile, contentious episode, especially in the morning before you go fishing, can put a serious damper on even the best-planned trip. More challenging is the boat partner or co-angler who demonstrates throughout the day that he doesn't know how to constructively cope with distressful feelings. It's pretty easy to feel discouraged or emotionally deflated when the day starts with an irritable, hostile, sarcastic, or insulting interchange.

In most areas of life, the best solution for dealing with such people is to walk away. Self-defense experts tell you to avoid conflict whenever you can. However, as much as you may want to, it's probably not a good idea to tie your nasty co-angler to a tree and then, *if you remember,* go back and pick him up at the end of the day! It's also usually not a good idea to just snap back at irritable club members, tournament staff, or sponsor personnel on whom you depend for financial support.

Situations vs. People

If you only get one thing out of this chapter, make it be this: learn to differentiate difficult people from reasonable people who are in a bad mood. Put another way, try to recognize the difference between problem people and problem situations. Most of us are grumpy, frustrated, or out of sorts on occasion, so being in a lousy mood doesn't necessarily mean someone is a bad person. If you show up at the dock excited, pumped up, and ready for a great day only to find your boat partner acting sullen and snotty, start by giving the person the benefit of the doubt. Assume this is probably a decent individual who is upset or worried about something in particular. Quickly jumping to the conclusion that this person must be a jerk leaves you with relatively few options.

The first marital arts class I took with my then-young daughter Ellen was memorable. Sure, I'd seen some Kung-Fu movies, and I think Chuck Norris is a talented guy! However, I was amazed to find that for *every* routine, the first step was *back*! Consider conflict resolution a form of self-defense and adopt this same philosophy. Think about it: stepping back as the *first* move gives you a wider picture, and time to size up the situation. For example, backing up may make it obvious that Mr. Crabby Co-Angler is upset about a broken piece of equipment.

Ask, Listen, Then Talk

If the issue isn't clear, consider using this four letter approach: **A-L-T-T**. These stand for Ask, Listen, Then Talk. Begin by saying something simple like "What's up?" or "How's it goin'?" That may be all it takes for a co-angler to tell you what's wrong. If a general question doesn't work, try the "Is there anything I can do to help?" approach. Most people who are having a tough time are not looking for a fight. By making it known you would rather be helpful than do battle, you'll be surprised at how fast some people become cooperative and agreeable.

You can use this same maneuver as a general practice with boat partners or fellow competitors to avoid *potential* conflicts. Begin your day by asking your boat partner or co-angler what he wants to do, and how you can be helpful to him. Just because he says something, doesn't mean you have to do it. However, showing initial interest in your co-angler significantly increases the likelihood that he will be cooperative and helpful to you.

In most instances, however, asking a few questions is just a good start. You also need to listen carefully to what the other person tells you. And pay attention to both the words your co-angler uses, and to the tone of voice he presents. I can't say that listening will help diffuse every situation because it doesn't always work (nothing *always* works, right?), but I will tell you that asking people how they are doing or what's wrong, and then *not* listening can easily make things worse.

Buy Some Time

If you still have a few moments to walk back to your truck, or go to the restroom, or chat with someone else on the dock, do it. Disengage from the conversation with a distressed individual and ask yourself these questions: What's going on? Why is this person upset? What are my options? This last question is particularly helpful to think about. Also, if you have a few moments and cell phone reception is good, make a call and ask a friend for ideas.

Once you have asked questions, listened carefully, and considered your options, then decide if you *want* to speak up. Sometimes, as Dr. Sherman illustrated, the best thing to say is nothing. If you have some ideas, offering advice or suggestions may seem like the thing to do. Alternately, there may be *nothing* you or anyone else can do at the moment, though there may be some assistance you could offer for a later time.

However, before the day starts, let your boat partner know what you want to have happen, and also state clearly what you want from him. Make it a point to be direct, calm, and succinct. Individuals who are upset typically aren't looking for lectures from someone who isn't. It's worth repeating: a good first strategy when dealing with a distressed person is to see if there isn't a problem the two of you could solve together.

119

The Genuinely Difficult Person

Of course, there are some people who are categorically not nice. Psychology uses diagnostic criteria to describe such people, and they are among the most challenging types of individuals to work with or change. If you are stuck for a day in a boat with such a person, you may find that almost nothing you say or do will help; in some cases, your offers of assistance may be turned against you! If you are a religious person, you could think of this as punishment for the bad things you did and got away with when you were a kid! Alternately, you could think of it as a human example of really bad weather. No one looks forward to fishing in twenty-five mile per hour wind, but there are some days when you have to do just that. So, no matter if it's the person in the back of your boat or the weather that's miserable, remember: this trip too, will eventually end!

And finally, here's something you can take to the bank: if you decide to confront or challenge an angry, upset, nasty individual, there is a *high* likelihood that you will be responded to in the same way. It's like this: "Why is it a bad idea to get into a mud wrestling contest with a pig? Because you will get very dirty, you will probably lose, and.........THE PIG LIKES IT!"

So, instead, ask questions, listen, offer suggestions, and admit when you are wrong. Trying to help rather than argue with people who are upset is clearly the better option.

REGULAR GUY TIP

So maybe you don't have a lot of patience for people who are in a bad mood, but you'd just as soon just let it go as deal with it. If your boat partner is upset or teed off, you just try to ignore him and act like it doesn't bother you. Well, at the very least, hang on to those three questions you read earlier, "What is going on?", "Why is this person upset?", and "What are my options?" They're useful questions to toss out the next time one of your fishing pals gets into a tangle with *his* co-angler!

CHAPTER 22

Use A Coach:
Everyone Else Does!

In the world of performance psychology, there aren't many things we can say for sure, but here's one of them: top competitors in every sport, *except fishing*, use a coach! Kobe Bryant has a coach. So does Peyton Manning. Even Dale Earnhardt Jr. and Kyle Petty learned at the feet of masters. So, doesn't it just make sense that if you want to be a great angler *you* should have a coach? However, most people who carry a rod and reel, including competitive fishing types, have not yet embraced this idea.

It's puzzling, really, since every angler I've ever talked with has been involved in some type of organized individual or team activity prior to taking up tournament fishing. Have you ever heard of a debate team, a band, a football squad, or a woodworking class that didn't have a teacher/coach/mentor handing out daily instructions and guidance? Still, when anglers talk about a coach or mentor, they usually refer to Dad, Aunt Clara, or the Old Timer At The Lake who provided early inspiration and instruction. After that, skill development typically took place via a series of individual trial and error episodes complimented by informal, catch-as-catch-can discussions with club members, tournament colleagues, or guys at the dock. In recent years books and videotapes have helped individual anglers learn on their own.

However, self-instruction is only one way to learn, and both experience and psychological research tell us self-instruction is not efficient. Sure, you want to figure out a unique approach that works for you, and that's fine, though ignoring hands-on instruction, face-to-face demonstrations, and the collective wisdom and expertise of seasoned veterans is a mistake. Over-relying on self-instruction increases the likelihood of avoidable mistakes and dead-ends, and it often leads to the frustration of having to relearn new skills over and over again.

Perhaps most significantly there is the risk of teaching yourself bad habits that later need to be unlearned. A Florida guide once gave me a graphic (and hilarious!) demonstration of what it was like trying to teach someone

121

to use a bait casting outfit. The "student" had gone to the ocean as a youngster and watched surf-casters do their thing. Based on what he remembered them doing he had "taught" himself an over-the-shoulder, two-handed technique that, with a bait-casting set up, consistently pounded lures into the water about three feet from the boat. (Here, try the visualization technique you learned in **Chapter 14** and give yourself a good laugh!) "His technique was so ingrained that even though I demonstrated over and over again how he should use his wrist as a lever, this guy just couldn't work it out," the angler told me.

Think about coaching in the same way you think about learning a new lake. On a new body of water you buy and use a map, right? It makes no sense to try to figure out the contours of a lake on your own if someone else has already done it, *and* done it better than you would have. Think of skill development with a coach the same way. If you can learn from an expert about a specific technique, why not do it?

Skill Development

A coach can do several things for you. To begin with, a coach can offer suggestions, ideas, or techniques you might not have thought of yourself. You may think you know all there is to know about sonar interpretation, for example, though an hour with a sonar expert might lead to a different conclusion. Of course, maybe you *do* know everything about your sonar, in which case an hour with a sonar expert would confirm that! A few years back, the drop shot technique came East, and some anglers took the opportunity to let their West Coast colleagues teach them. It was a great chance for veteran anglers to demonstrate their commitment to skill development and collaborative learning. Adopting that same attitude opens the door to input from a coach or mentor!

Feedback Again

I've already talked about the importance of getting clear, accurate feedback. It's almost impossible to accurately monitor your own performance *while* you are fishing. A coach will notice and comment on things about your technique that you don't see. Research repeatedly documents the near-universal tendency of individuals to overestimate their skills and accomplishments. A coach can be objective, realistic, and instructive with feedback in instances where you cannot.

Inspiration and Support

A coach can, as the song says, "Clear a path or light the flame". You already know how difficult it is to pick yourself up after a lousy day on the water, or after a bad tournament. Coach can help restore your energy, give encouragement, and get you back in the saddle when you can't do it yourself. Of course, it is quickly apparent that many fishermen, especially tournament fishermen are remarkably resilient. They have to be. There are no guarantees in fishing, and it's not hard to go from first to last on the leaderboard. However, even the most psychologically solid, confident, well-adjusted individuals will have tough days. Climbing the steps to the weigh-in stage with an empty bag is no fun. And a prolonged slump or dry spell can be emotionally draining to anyone. Coach can help focus, re-energize, and in some cases re-direct an angler who has gotten off track.

Be a Pioneer

This is a very interesting era in the evolution of competitive fishing. Our sport is barely one generation old. For the first time in its brief history, tournament fishing has individuals with enough experience, wisdom, and knowledge to take on the role of coach. Initially, tournaments were a loose affiliation of fiercely independent, self-reliant anglers who had no choice but to learn by themselves. These were true pioneers, individuals who turned away from mainstream occupations and secure careers to explore what was then only a dream and a hope. Now these individuals are heroes, the figureheads in the sport of tournament fishing. And one of them could become your mentor!

You, on the other hand, have the opportunity to be another kind of pioneer. Since there aren't many true "fishing coaches" out there, it may take some time, energy, and initiative to find a technique expert who's willing to be your coach. Instead of one coach, you may end up with two or more individuals who provide specific rather than general instruction. Fishing clinics and classes are worth exploring, though nothing beats individualized, one-on-one instruction.

If you have ever coached yourself, you have the same priceless memories the rest of us have of seeing new-found techniques become part of a student's repertoire. The smiles of appreciation, and those heart-felt words, "Thanks Coach" remind us that coaching works!

But seriously, if Tiger Woods has a coach, why don't you?

123

REGULAR GUY TIP

I can hear you now "I don't want no fishin' coach, all I wanna do is catch me a few more bass or walleyes or crappies or bream or whatever." Fine! Well, you're not too old to learn, are you? Try this: Who's the best fisherman on your lake/river? Where does he have coffee in the mornin'? (You don't know? Well, for cryin' out loud, find out! There's only a few places he *could* be havin' coffee.) And where does he stop for a cold one in the afternoon? (Follow him and see!) Once you know, go to those places when he's likely to be there, and just hang out. Do it a few times. Get so he recognizes you, if he don't already. Then take one of your buddies with you, and sit where Mr. Local Expert can overhear you. Don't talk to him directly. Instead start talkin' fishin' to your buddy, but make it clear that you're only catchin' a few. After about three or four times, this guy won't be able to stand it; pretty soon he'll feel compelled to **be** Mr. Local Expert, and then he'll lean over and make a comment or two about what you *should* be doin'. I've seen this happen, and so have you. And if Mr. Local Expert turns out to be my dad, tell him I said "Hi".

CHAPTER 23

Can a Sport Psychologist Help Someone Like Me?

In the last chapter I talked about finding a technique coach. This chapter is about getting a mental coach. Top athletes often have one of each. I already said this, but I'll say it again; *decades* of research in several sports have shown that performance psychology techniques, used correctly, enhance effectiveness. In most cases, skills develop best under the guidance of a trained mentor. With that idea in mind, let me suggest you meet with a performance psychologist, at least to see if it helps.

Self-Awareness

Self-awareness is a lot like fishing (isn't everything a lot like fishing?!?!). In general, the more you know about fishing the more successful you will be, right? Similarly, the more you know about yourself psychologically, the better off you'll be. In over thirty years of doing psychological evaluations, I have conservatively assessed some fifteen thousand people. However, I have yet to meet the individual who fully and accurately understands all his or her strengths and weaknesses. Each of us has tendencies, preferences, attitudes, beliefs, and behavior patterns we do not completely recognize or understand. Certainly the self-awareness/self-understanding exercises in this book can get you started in the right direction. However, a good sport psychologist can take you even further down this road.

Our best psychological assessment tools have been around for more than fifty years, and if you complete them in an honest way, you'll get detailed, insightful information about your personality, your learning style, and your coping strategies. Interviews, questionnaires, and test batteries can create a full, comprehensive picture of an individual's psychological makeup. It's like using sonar. A Lowrance "Green Box" can give you *some* helpful underwater information, though today's liquid crystal sonar/lake map/GPS units give so much more! The more detailed and accurate your map (of the lake, of yourself) the more you will likely make good decisions and adaptive choices.

Technique Development

Chapters on relaxation skills, concentration techniques, visualization methods, mental rehearsal, stress management, optimal intensity, and confidence all included exercises that, with perseverance and practice, will provide significant benefits. However, as the discussion in **Chapter 19** indicates, putting it all together in a **Psychological Tackle Box** will be more efficient with the help of an instructor. Additionally, a sport psychologist can help you experiment with different variations of these techniques until the ones that are most effective emerge. One of the first techniques I learned from a sport psychologist was how to not make a bad situation worse, something I was inclined to do in my younger days when I was even more excitable that I am now! Backlashes were a particular sore spot for me, and I would often compound the tangled line with an emotional outburst that was not, shall we say, polite, or brief!

Everyone knows it's easier to pick out a backlash under calm circumstances than when anger and aggravation rule, and my psychologist helped me figure out strategies to help remain poised when my line snarled. After several practice sessions, I had an on-the-water opportunity to use what I had learned. I was dock fishing with my son Patrick when the line on my *spinning reel* went ka-flooey. He laughed of course, which normally would have made me all the madder, but I tried to remember what my coach said. I laughed back, I joked that "backlashes need love, too" and finally untangled my line. Then I *carefully* picked up the slack ....and set the hook! I wish you could have seen the look on my son's face when I landed the three pounder! Guess who was laughing hysterically then! That *never* would have happened if I had not gotten that specific tip and training from a sport psychologist.

Systematic Learning

Learning theory is a section of psychology that has clear, well-documented guiding principles. Learning principles are part of the bedrock of my profession, and a good sport psychologist can help you set up a learning schedule that includes goals, specific steps, action plans and time frames, as well as check points for monitoring progress. Look at using a sport psychologist in the same light as having a personal trainer or a strength coach. Sure, there are lots of machines and weight systems in the gym, though it's easy to waste time randomly trying this one and that one. A good psychological coach will help you discover which mental exercises are best for you, and provide expert guidance along the way.

Be Skeptical

Not all sport psychologists are created equal. It goes without saying that it pays to be a smart consumer; however, I would go further and say be a skeptical critic should you decide to enlist the services of a performance psychologist. Check credentials, get references, and ask around in the community. If you are unsure about how to find a sport psychologist, call the psychology department at your local university and ask to speak to the clinical director. The person in charge of psychological training at the university likely knows several local professionals, and you may get information about who has a good reputation and who does not. In the end, trust your own feelings when it comes to evaluating professionals. Give yourself three sessions to see if the two of you are on the same wavelength. If you are, fine; if not, find someone else!

The Myth of Mental Discipline

Just don't fool yourself into thinking that instead of a sport psychologist what you primarily need is more personal discipline. I can't tell you how many times I've heard people complain about wishing they had more discipline. "You know Doc, if I was just more disciplined, I would be able to _____." Fill in the blank with *any* activity you want, and somebody has said that sentence!

However, it is my contention that personal discipline is overrated. Yeah, I know there are some people out there who are extraordinarily self-directed, self-motivated, and self-disciplined. You may know someone who creates and executes plans like clockwork. You may even know a few anglers who are extraordinarily well-prepared, conscientious, and consistent. Naturally disciplined individuals, like my fishing pal Tom, are few and far between, however.

Tom was a star athlete. He held a number of state high school track records in Iowa......for a long time. After high school, Tom went off to college and then to medical school. There was a residency in psychiatry and then a headfirst dive into a time-consuming medical career. In there somewhere he got married and had a couple of kids. But he never gave up being an athlete. He didn't much care what the sport was, if it involved a workout, Tom did it. Tennis, broomball, golf, racquetball, basketball in the driveway, canoeing down nameless rivers in Alaska, you name it; if he hadn't grown up in Iowa, he probably would have been a heck of a hockey player! One by one his athletic partners dropped off as middle-age took them out, but Tom just switched over to individual sports like running, rollerblading, and cross-country skiing. To keep himself challenged, he signed up for marathons, and half marathons, and 5 and 10K races. And so there he was on our annual Canadian walleye trip, well past fifty, standing on a dock in Nowheresville, Ontario waiting for the floatplane, wearing his high school letter jacket that still fit like the day he got it!

But, I promise you, do not try to be like Tom! Why not? Answer this question: can you run a hundred meters in less than ten seconds? I thought so. Neither can I. It wouldn't make much sense for you or me to get into a race against people who could, would it? More importantly, if you are not naturally built like a world class sprinter, *no amount* of conditioning, weight training, or "self-discipline" will allow you to break ten seconds in a hundred meter race! Similarly, striving for greater mental or personal discipline is most likely an exercise in futility. Trying to force yourself to become the disciplined person you are not will, as it probably has the past, lead to recurrent frustration.

When people talk to me about wanting greater self-discipline, they typically are not interested in more discipline itself. Instead, what they really want is more consistency in one area of life or another. But you don't need spectacular self-discipline to become consistent. Most people who are consistent have put together a set of circumstances and healthy habits that end up looking like mental discipline.

Think about this from your own experience. Remember back in high school or maybe grade school when you played in the band or competed on a sport's team? There, the path to success included a practice book, a practice schedule, and a lot of other people to practice with. While some individual effort was required, most practice sessions were conducted in a group setting. Additionally, besides teammates you had social support from friends and family, and there was also an involved teacher or coach or two, or three! In this setting, with repeated practice, your skill level and your performance improved. What a surprise! Without exceptional "self-discipline", a system run by a mentor caused you to be successful. So is the culprit behind inconsistent performance really lack of self-discipline? I don't think so. If someone had handed you a trumpet in the third grade without systems, routines, teachers, and schedules, it is *extremely* unlikely that you would have ended up first chair in the high school jazz band.

Fast forward to today, and your fishing career. Whether or not you fish tournaments, look at what you now expect yourself to do: perform tedious, joyless tasks, work alone, and with little structure, and learn new techniques with minimal guidance and inconsistent social support. What would you rather do—fish or clean your reels? Drive around the lake and look for cover and structure, or vacuum and wash your boat? Well, Duh!!

So what's an angler to do? Use a sport psychologist, that's what. A performance psychologist will help you master tasks that are intrinsically rewarding, and also show you how to cope with unpleasant tasks that are not. A sport psychologist can be your guide as you develop routines, manage your time efficiently, and develop practice schedules. Besides teaching you the action steps outlined in **Chapters 12-18**, a sport psychologist will walk you through the exercises in **Chapters 1-4.**

Since I don't know you personally, I can't tell you which of those chapters will be the most meaningful, though a sport psychologist who gets to know you will!

REGULAR GUY TIP

There is no *possible way* you, as a Regular Guy, are gonna get talked into gettin' onto a sport psychologist's couch, so I'm not even going to try. And besides, a sport psychologist will charge you about $150 an hour, which around here will keep you and your buddies in beer and minnows all summer long. So, go ahead; buy the beer and minnows instead. You were gonna do that anyway. Just remember to drink responsibly, and if you get hungry, eat the minnows one at a time, rather than by the handful!

CHAPTER 24

Begin Again:
Using "Do-Over" As a Fishing Technique

At some point, either by the calendar or by the tournament season, one fishing year comes to an end or another one begins. However you determine it, the end of the year is a good time to step back and Review, Renew, and Revise. Regardless of how well or how poorly *this* year went, next year is a "Do Over". Your psychological well-being will benefit, and your fishing will likely improve if you annually do your inventory. I suggest January because that is what most anglers I work with prefer, but feel free to use whatever timeframe feels best.

Review

When it comes to your annual review, go back to **Chapter 1** and read through your commitments and priorities. Are those still aligned and balanced? Check with the people around you to make sure you answer this question correctly!

Then consider the practical skills list in **Chapter 2**. Congratulate yourself on what you improved. Flip through the exercises on keeping track and managing time. What worked well this year? What didn't?

Also, spend some time on your long range, short-term, and immediate goals. Look at the parts of goal-setting that worked best. Also, consider visiting a sport psychologist to make even more powerful goals and plans for next season. Additionally, ask yourself if it's time to tweak a couple routines, and add to or modify your mental strengthening techniques.

As you review your skills and talents, and make plans to do better next year, let me remind you of the importance of being candid and honest about what you know, what you have(talents) and what you can do(skills). In preparing to write this book, I talked with or interviewed many competitive as well as noncompetitive anglers, guys who pursue this sport on several levels. When asked to describe the most common mental mistake fishermen make these anglers all said the same thing: "They overestimate what they can do." Try not to inflate your skills just to make yourself feel better. It will cost you in the long run.

Renew

After reviewing your priorities and goals, come up with a sentence or two that expresses a renewed dedication to your fishing career. Try sentences like, "This year will be my best year", or "I will be even more determined this season". You'll get the most benefit out of this by writing your renewed commitments down and telling other people about them.

Revise

As you look at what worked well last year and what didn't, consider the concept of challenging yourself. No one else is around to grade your performance! You will have to do that on your own. However, you will be ahead of the competition if you create internal as well as external challenges for the coming year. From an external standpoint, you could challenge yourself to move higher in the point standings for your club or circuit. You could also challenge yourself to improve an external skill such as distancing yourself from dock talk, learning more about your GPS, or being more consistent with equipment maintenance. You certainly could challenge yourself to keep better records than you did last year!

Internally you might challenge yourself to try a new mental strengthening technique. Let's say visualization worked well for you last year. Perhaps in the coming year it would be worthwhile to experiment with mental rehearsal, or with one of the stress management techniques outlined in **Chapter 16**. Alternately, you could think about the worst mental mistake you made last year, and ask a sport psychologist what would be the best way to keep *that* from happening again.

Anticipate Obstacles

Failure to anticipate likely obstacles is one of the main reasons personal challenges fail and goals remain unmet. Good record-keeping will allow you to effectively review last year, notice the most challenging obstacles, and put plans in place to minimize or circumvent them in the coming season. For goals, plans, and techniques, however, try using this sequence: What? When? Where? How? *and*, What is the most likely obstacle I will face?

Ask for Help

A fishing coach and/or a sport psychologist can make a big difference, as I've said. Even if you decide not to go this route, find a way to get some help from *someone* for the coming season. Read a couple of new fishing books, take an idea from a magazine article and build a practice plan, or incorporate the specifics of a video into your fishing arsenal. Remember, the greatest athletes, at the top of their game, continuously ask for help in an open-minded, humble, I-can-learn-from-anyone kind of way.

The best example of this I have ever witnessed came from the guy who wrote the preface to my book: Denny Brauer. We were practice fishing for a tournament in Alabama, working our way down a chunk rock bank. Not wanting to fish behind Denny with exactly the same bait as his, I tied on an obscure brown-and-something jig as we pitched the rocks. We had been fishing for a couple of hours and not much was happening. Suddenly Denny said, "You've got a bite!" Sure enough! My line had moved several feet off the bank, *all by itself*! Too late, I set the hook, but only had him for three cranks before he got off—just long enough for him to swirl on the surface. I started paying closer attention. About fifteen minutes later, my line jumped again, and this time I was ready. I set the hook, got him to the boat, and just as I reached down to pick him up, he bailed out. Great!! I'm 0 for 2!

I will be in a nursing home with late stage Alzheimer's, no longer able to remember my own name, before I forget what happened next. Denny Brauer turned around, walked to the back of the boat, and said "Let me see that jig you're using." I thought to myself, "What in the name of All Creation is Denny Brauer doing looking at *my* jig?!?" And then it hit me. *This* is the reason he has won more money fishing than anybody. As great as he is, he *still* wants to learn. He doesn't care if I'm Donald Duck! If I've got a bait the fish are eating, Denny wants to know what it is!

How Long Will It Take?

If you have been fishing tournaments for a while, and especially if you are a seasoned veteran, this **Begin Again** philosophy probably seems reasonable. You have come to appreciate that every year is a new year, every tournament a new tournament. In each event, everyone starts out tied for first. Looking ahead, there are fish to be caught, reputations to be built or diminished, and careers to be made. Without a doubt, this *is* a

132

race, as George said, and stopping too long to rest is a bad idea because there are other people running behind you who want nothing more than to pass you on the leaderboard. But you know this, and so you will Review last year's performance, Renew your commitments, and make some Revisions. What doesn't work will get changed next year.

However, if you're new to fishing, especially competitive fishing, **Begin Again** might not make any sense at all. In fact, it might seem stupid. You may be thinking what I've heard other anglers say: "I did all that stuff. I set goals, I worked hard, and I tried new things. And most of the time I sucked. And now you want me to begin again? How long will this take?" Well, there isn't anything genuinely helpful to say here. The canned and also correct answer is: "It takes as long as it takes," but that just sounds like dribble to the struggling new angler. However, even if the term Frustrated Rookie applies, I will still recommend that you do what top professionals do: use the Review, Renew, Revise sequence, get some help, and challenge yourself to **Begin Again**.

But before the season starts, do this as well. Contact three or four anglers who have been around the block, and ask each of them to tell you their story. Hear what they went through when they were first getting started. Listen to them recount frustrating tournament after frustrating tournament. And ask them your question, "How long does it take?" You won't get a good answer from them either, not one that will make this year any easier, but what you will get is their honest answer, and if you put all of those answers together, what you will have is something that sounds like this: "It takes a while, some times more than a while, but brother, it's worth it!"

Of course, I could duck the "How long will it take?" question by saying "Well, just enjoy the journey, appreciate the friends you make, and learn something everyday", though that probably sounds trite to you. Those things are all true, by the way. My closest friends in all the world are the people I fish with. And most of the spectacular images of Mother Nature I have tucked away were seen from the deck of a boat.

But I won't lie: in the end, it *is* about catching fish. *The most* spectacular moment was cashing that first check! At least it *was* the most spectacular moment until I won my first partner tournament, which was *by far* the most wonderful thing on earth, until I won an individual event, and that couldn't *possibly* be topped by anything else, except *it was*, three weeks later, when I won again, this time with a six fish limit that weighed over twenty-two pounds.

How long did it take? A long time!

Was it worth it?

From the bottom of my heart..........YES!